STRUCTURE AND PERFORMANCE RELATIONSHIP IN INDIAN INDUSTRIES

About the Author

Maninder Singh Sarkaria is a Lecturer at District Institute of Education and Training, Amritsar. Earlier, he worked as a Lecturer in Commerce.

Dr. Sarkaria earned his PG.degree from Guru Nanak Dev University, Amritsar for his work in the field of industrial economics. He has contributed several papers to journals of national and international repute.

STRUCTURE AND PERFORMANCE RELATIONSHIP IN INDIAN INDUSTRIES

Maninder Singh Sarkaria

CONCEPT PUBLISHING COMPANY, NEW DELHI-110059

Cataloging in Publication Data—DK
Courtesy: D.K. Agencies (P) Ltd. <docinfo@dkagencies.com>

Sarkaria, Maninder Singh, 1967-
Structure and performance relationship in Indian industries / Maninder Singh Sarkaria.
p. ; cm.
Includes bibliographical references (p.)
Includes index.
ISBN 8180691756

1. Industries—India. 2. Manufacturing industries—India. 3. Business enterprises—India. I. Title.

DDC 338.009 54 21

ISBN 81-8069-175-6

First Published 2005

Published and Printed by
Ashok Kumar Mittal
Concept Publishing Company
A/15-16, Commercial Block, Mohan Garden
NEW DELHI-110059 (India)

Phones : 25351460, 25351794
Fax : +91-11-25357103
Email : publishing@conceptpub.com

PREFACE

In the modern business world of razor-sharp competition, resources are used so carefully and thoughtfully as to give the maximum returns. And the presence of differential performance is attributed to various impediments to resource flows. The study of such impediments has been the principal concern of Industrial Organisation economists as well as of the Strategic Management scholars. In industrial organisation, market structure has long been considered as a primary determinant of industrial performance. The work in this field has sought to identify factors which influence corporate economic performance. Important industrial characteristics which have been used by the researchers in this field as the determinants of financial performance are : concentration, market share, industry growth, research and development expenditure, advertisement intensity and the size of firms in industry. On the other hand, the strategic management, often called 'policy' or simply 'strategy' has been concerned about the direction of the organisations or the business firms. The researchers in this field have used firm-specific variables to explain performance differences. The selection of firm's goals, the choice of products and services offered by the firm, the diversification policy and administrative structure of firm, the size, leverage, risk, age, skill, capital intensity of the firm are some of the determinants of performance in strategic management research. Until some years ago, industrial economists and strategic management scholars have been working independently in their respective fields to ascribe meaning to the observed performance differentials or to the variables that correlate with performance. In the recent past, strategic management scholars have been using the language and logic of economics to interpret their findings. In the other direction, some economists are positioning their work as relevant to general managers.

A review of the literature on this subject reveals that most of the work in this area has been undertaken in industrially advanced countries, notably in United States. Far less attention has been paid in this area in less developed countries (LDCs). India being one of the largest developing countries, provides good ground for such study. But surprisingly, there are only a few studies in India which have been conducted to analyse the determinants of dispersion in inter-industry performance. Taking profitability and growth as the twin indicators of composite performance, this study has sought to investigate and interpret performance differentials among various industries in India. In the light of the cross-over between the fields of industrial organisation and strategic management as mentioned above, performance differential aspects have been examined taking into consideration both the viewpoints. Appropriate statistical models have been developed to systematically examine the impact of various factors on performance of companies operating in various manufacturing and non-manufacturing industries.

The book is likely to be useful for the students of industrial economics, strategic management and business policy in general and for the researchers of Indian corporate sector, corporate executives and prospective entrepreneurs in particular. The methodology developed in this work to study market structure-performance relationship is being used by the researchers in other fields also.

This book is based on my doctoral thesis submitted to Guru Nanak Dev University, Amritsar. I deem it a matter of privilege to express my profound sense of respect to my supervisor, Dr. G.S. Shergill, formerly Professor of Guru Nanak Dev University, Amritsar and presently associated with Massey University, Auckland, New Zealand for his invaluable guidance and constructive criticism to complete this research work. I am equally grateful to Dr. H.S. Sidhu, Professor of Economics, Guru Nanak Dev University, Amritsar for encouraging and guiding me especially during the times of my supervisor's long stays abroad. I am indebted to Prof. G.K. Chadha, presently Vice Chancellor, Jawaharlal Nehru University, New Delhi who helped me in ways more than one to accomplish this task. I am also thankful to my colleagues Mrs. Madhu Sharma and Principal J.S. Nagpal, for helping me in one way or the other to carry out this work successfully.

My special thanks are also due to the Concept Publishing Company, New Delhi for doing a great job of bringing out this book. My wife Sharan, kids Jagmohit and Mannat, and friends also deserve special thanks for their co-operation at every stage of this work.

Maninder Singh Sarkaria

CONTENTS

LIST OF TABLES

LIST OF FIGURES

ABBREVIATIONS USED

ADV INT.	Advertising Intensity
ANOVA	Analysis of Variance
A.R.E.	Arab Republic of Egypt
ASI	Annual Survey of Industries
Bn	Billion
C.V.	Coefficient of Variation
CMIE	Centre for Monitoring Indian Economy
CR4	Four Firm Concentration Ratios
EPS	Earnings Per Share
FTC	Federal Trade Commission
GDIV	Growth in Dividend
GNP	Gross National Product
GRT	Gross Registered Tonnage
GRTH	Growth
GSALES	Growth in Sales
GTNA	Growth in Total Net Assets
HEB	High Entry Barriers
HI	Herfindahl Index
HSD	Honestly Significant Difference
IND.	Industry
I.O.	Industrial Organisation
ISIC	International Standard Industrial Classification
JPC	Joint Plan Committee
Kgs	Kilograms
KW.	Kilowatt
LB	Line of Business
LDCs	Less Developed Countries
MEB	Medium Entry Barriers
MEC	Minimum Economic Capacity
MES	Minimum Efficient Scale

Mn	Million
MRTP	Monopolies and Restrictive Trade Practices
MS	Market Share
NDP	Net Domestic Product
NIC	National Industrial Classification
No.	Number
OLS	Ordinary Least Squares
P	Profit
PCM	Price-Cost Margin
PIMS	Profit Impact of Market Strategy
PLF	Plant Load Factor
PRTF	Profitability
RBI	Reserve Bank of India
R&D	Research and Development
ROA	Return on Assets
ROCE	Return on Capital Employed
ROE	Return on Equity
ROS	Return on Sales
SEBs	State Electricity Boards
SEOD	Stock Exchange Official Directory
SIC	Standard Industrial Classification
SMP	Statutory Minimum Price
SCP	Structure-Conduct-Performance
SP	Structure-Performance
UK	United Kingdom
US	United States
USA	United States of America
USSR	Union of Soviet Socialist Republics
VIF	Variance Inflation Factor

1

INTRODUCTION

Background of the Study

Needless to pinpoint that various impediments to resource flows result in performance differentials and, therefore, necessitate cautious and sagacious exploitation of the available resources so as to maximise dividends, specially in the ongoing cut-throat competitive business world. The study of such impediments as are the root cause of performance differentials, has been the principal concern of the industrial organisation economics. In industrial organisation economics, following Bain (1951, 1956), industry has been the unit of analysis. The works in this field have sought to identify factors which influence corporate economic performance. It has been persistently shown that firms in a particular industry earn comparatively above normal profits because of some favourable structural characteristics. The main features which indicate the market structure are concentration and concentration ratios, product differentiation, barriers to entry of new firms, growth rate of market demand, price elasticity of market demand etc. Many studies have revealed that some structural variables allow firms in some industries to be in a better position to implement their strategies successfully and profitably.

In contrast to industrial organisation economics, strategic management researchers have studied the causes of differential performance from a very different perspective. They have sought to relate corporate economic performance to the unique endowment and actions of individual corporations or business units. The problem of persistent profits has been taken up on both the fronts. Both of these research fields ascribe different meanings to performance differentials between groups, or to variables that correlate with performance. Strategy research links the persistent performance differences to efficiency, difficult-to-imitate resources etc. The industrial organisation economics, on the other hand, puts forth the explanation for abnormal returns in terms of entry barriers, scale economies etc.

Interestingly the importance of industry membership has been realised equally by the researchers from both the fields. Montgomery (1979) has revealed that the structure of the industries in which the firm participates and the competitive position of the firm's business in each industry are the major determinants of the performance. Porter (1980) asserts that the characteristics of the various industries in which a firm competes and the position of the firm's business in these industries influence the overall firm performance. Porter (1985) reports that not all industries offer equal opportunities for sustained profitability. Many researchers have stated that industry effects explained a significant portion of the variation in the company profitability (Schmalensee, 1985; Kessides, 1990; Amato and Wilder, 1990)*. Schmalensee (1989) has argued that inter-industry research can help to formulate sound theory and facilitate empirical testing of specific industries.

There is no denying the fact that industrialisation plays a critical role in the process of economic development and industrialisation has been a fundamental objective of most developing countries. In such countries, industrial development is considered necessary to achieve high rate of economic growth and to provide for the basic needs of the population. The studies on industries can reflect the performance of the economy of a country and provide vital information for policy making. However, a review of the empirical studies on inter-industries on profit variation reveals that most of the work in this area has been undertaken in industrially advanced countries, notably in the United States. Far less attention has been paid to the analysis of industrial structure, behaviour and policy in developing countries.

---

* We will discuss these studies in subsequent chapters.

India being one of the largest developing countries, provides a good ground for such study. Nevertheless, surprisingly, there seems to be a few studies which have been conducted in India to analyse the determinants of dispersion in inter-industry profitability. All of them differ from one another in respect of scope, time periods and variables used and are suffering from one or the other handicap. Gupta (1968) used single year profit data of 1958 while Siddharthan and Dasgupta (1983) covered a period of three-years (1975-76 to 1977-78). Such a short run data is not considered appropriate to test a long run relationship and also such a short span does not capture the overall business cycle effects. Walgreen (1971) simply analysed Gupta's data with a different methodology and inherited all its shortcomings. Further more, the time period of Siddharthan and Dasgupta's study, more or less, coincides with the national emergency in which there was a complete control of the government on the economy of the country. Further this study was conducted for the period 1975-76 to 1977-78, but since then, a lot of changes have taken place. Except Siddharthan and Dasgupta, all the studies used industry as the unit of analysis. However, the company-based study of profitability is considered to provide more complete and qualitative results. In the light of the above-mentioned factors, it was thought that a comprehensive study covering all these aspects be carried out. This study is aimed to achieve this.

Objectives of the Study

The major objective of the study is to investigate the performance differences among various industries in India. The specific objectives of this study are to study the performance differences among various industries *vis-à-vis* their profitability as well as in terms of growth. The market structure-performance relationship will also be investigated.

A composite measure of performance has been employed that incorporates profitability and growth dimensions of performance. The two indicators of profitability used in the study are Return on Equity (ROE) and Return on Assets (ROA). The indicators of growth employed in this research work are Growth in Sales (GSALES), Growth in Dividend (GDIV) and Growth in Total Net Assets (GTNA).

Both a multi-industry and multi-company approach involving a sample of 187 large Indian companies in the manufacturing and non-manufacturing sector is used to investigate inter-industry performance differentials and to demonstrate the role of market structure variables in explaining performance differences across various industries. The 11-year period chosen for the study ranges from 1980-81 to 1990-91. The analysis has been carried out for three different classifications of industry, viz. Input-based classification, Used-based classification and Commodity/Activity-based classification.

The study has been confined to private sector only because public sector enterprises are different from the enterprises operating in the private sector and it may be unfair to compare the profitability of the units operating in these two different sectors. The data have been collected from the secondary sources only. The main sources used are various issues of the Stock Exchange Official Directory (SEOD) and publications of the Centre for Monitoring Indian Economy (CMIE).

Structure of the Book

For the sake of convenience the book has been chapterised to deal with the varied aspects of the study. The introducing chapter brings to light the background of the study and its objectives. Chapter 2 carries the review of literature on the empirical studies regarding performance differentials in India and abroad. The literature review has been grouped and discussed under the headings of industrial organisation economics and strategic management. The underlying data, the variables and the methodology used in the study are presented in Chapter 3. Chapter 4 reflects upon the viewpoint of industrial economists on the aspects of performance differentials and the discussion on various structural variables. In-depth analysis of performance differentials among various industry groups is taken up in Chapter 5. Chapter

6 provides a detailed investigation of the determinants of inter-industry performance dispersions. Chapter 7 scrutinises the strength of the relationship of various market structure variables with performance indicators. The concluding chapter is to epitomise the overall findings of the study, foresee its implications and find out the scope for further research.

2

LITERATURE REVIEW

This study attempts to analyse performance differentials and seeks to link the results to various factors. There are two schools of thought, which study and interpret performance differentials, viz. strategic management and industrial organisation economics. Both of these research fields ascribe different meanings to performance differentials between groups, or to variables that correlate with performance. The research on market share effect provides a good example. The empirical association between market share and profitability was first addressed in industrial organisation economics and their association was interpreted as "market power". As per the structure-conduct-performance framework, market share represented structure (conduct was implicit) and super profits were discerned as poor social performance. On the strategic management front, the market shares was seen as an asset that could be 'bought' or 'sold' for strategic purposes and the managers were advised to invest in shares in growing industries and withdraw from declining industries. Strategic management community carried on further research to estimate the 'cost' of gaining market share. Surprisingly no cost to share gains was found. Changes in share and changes in profitability were positively related in every context examined. However, when the analysis was carried out taking help from economic theory and advanced econometrics to further clarify this issue (share-profit association), the relationship was interpreted as causally spurious. Instead, an observed stochastic process (i.e. luck, good management) was jointly driving both share and profitability. Most of the work on market share-profitability relationship has been carried out within strategic management rather than by economists who had initiated work on this subject. Interestingly, industrial organisation economics and strategic management cross over between the fields and help to provide better insights into the problems. Certainly both the fields have benefited from each other. Certain strategy researchers have adopted the language and logic of economics, enabling them to reformulate economic theory [see, Porter's (1980) influential treatment of industry structure]. In the other direction, some economists, armed with new tools and richer theories, have attacked problems of central interest to strategic management, and have posit their work as relevant to general managers [see, Jensen's (1989) view on corporate control]. To take another example, the logic of experience-based competition was not imported from economics, but was instead developed within strategic management and then exported to economics.

The problem of persistent profits has been taken up on both the fronts. Strategy research links the persistent performance differences to efficiency, difficult-to-imitate resources etc. The industrial organisation economics, on the other hand, puts forth the explanation for abnormal returns in terms of entry barriers, scale economies etc. Hence, we see that the literature review on performance differentials can be divided into two categories. One, which consists of the studies, carried on in strategic management, the other comprising of the research work done within economics or more particularly in industrial organisation economics.

Literature Review in Strategic Management Research

Following the pioneering work of Chandler (1962) in the field of strategic management research, Rumelt (1974, 1977) examined the relationship among diversification strategy, organisational structure and economic performance. He developed nine categories of diversification and found that related diversification strategy outperformed the other diversification strategies, but he could not show the causes of dispersion in performance among various diversification strategies. However, he asserted that related diversified firms enjoyed superior returns because of their common skills or resources into related areas. He also indicated that each industry has different structural characteristics which have an impact on all the firms in that industry. Rumelt's (1974, 1977) work has been criticised because it did not control industry effects.

Bettis and Hall (1982) found no significant differences between related and unrelated diversified firms. Their results strongly suggested that much of the differences in performance between related and unrelated diversified firms in Rumelt's study was due to the presence of pharmaceutical companies in his sample and not to the diversified strategies *per se*. Following the criticism of his studies (1974, 1977), Rumelt (1982) extended the analysis by controlling the industry effects on performance. Here again he obtained the similar results but he identified that industry effect was primarily responsible for the high performance of related constrained firms.

Hamilton and Shergill (1993) carried a study on strategy, structure and performance in New Zealand quoted companies. In order to assess the impact of diversification strategies on performance, he included company size, leverage, risk, technical opportunity and industry participation as control variables in the model. They revealed the existence of industry effects and found them to be significant determinants of performance differentials. They showed that some group of industries earned comparatively lower rates of return. Furthermore, they reported that these industry effects have explained a substantial part of the company performance.

Montgomery (1985) analysed the association among diversification, market structure and firm performance. His sample consisted of 128 Fortune 500 firms. He revealed that high-diversified firms differed significantly from low-diversified firms. The low-diversified firms enjoyed high market power and were in stronger position. Moreover, firm performance was found positively associated with market share, market profitability and market growth.

Woo and Cooper (1982) argued that high market share was not always a key to profitability and low market share did not necessarily lead to low profits. Of the 126 businesses that they studied, 40 showed superior performance despite low market share.

They observed that relating high market share to high profitability was not always valid. They asserted that businesses with low market share could have experienced high profitability by focusing their attention on market environment, business strategies, product quality, price etc.

Jacobson and Aaker (1985) empirically investigated the relationship between market share and profitability. The findings revealed the influence of market share on profitability considerably lower than the ones widely reported in previous studies. They observed that unnecessarily high importance had been placed on market share as a determinant of profitability. They suggested that high market share alone should not be related to profitability. They listed other factors which could be equally or more important, viz. product quality, consumer satisfaction, productivity, corporate culture, product line appropriateness and management effectiveness.

Schwalbach (1991) empirically investigated the relationship between profitability and market share for 2744 business units. He divided the total sample into 8 different types of businesses. The results revealed that a critical market share existed between 65 and 70 per cent and beyond that level profitability declined. Additionally, in some types of businesses, small-share business units were as successful as the larger business units. Moreover, very large share business units were found less profitable.

Literature Review in Industrial Organisation Economics

Industrial organisation economists explain the causes of differences in performance from a very different perspective. They have used market structure variables to explain the differences in profitability across industries. In any economy, there are number of companies prevailing in different industries; and different industries have different structural characteristics resulting in different average industry profits. This is the central theme of industrial organisation economics and studies in this field involve statistical analysis of data from multiple industries and mostly focus on the determinant of profitability. Generally, a multiple regression equation is run across the data from multiple industries.

Studies in United States

As a harbinger, Bain (1951) was the first to find a link between profitability and concentration. His pioneering work was based on the US data for the period 1936-40. He selected 42 industries from amongst 340 industries (for which concentration ratios were computed) dropping those in respect of which data were either not available or unsuitable. He divided these 42 industries into two groups, one-consisting of the most concentrated industries having eight-firms concentration ratio above 70 per cent and the other group comprised of the rest of the industries representing the least concentrated industries. He found that average rate of return in the most concentrated industries was significantly higher than that of those operating in least concentrated group. The difference was statistically significant. Bain associated this relationship with successfully collusion between firms. Bain, however, did not draw any firm conclusion from his investigation and indicated that this significant difference between the two groups was subject to number of reservations. Bain's worked stimulated further research and a great number of studies proved the theory that there is a link between concentration and successful collusion. Bain (1956) showed that both concentration and barriers to entry were important determinants of performance in industries.

Stigler (1964) tried to test the hypothesis that oligopoly firms indulge in collusive practices in order to maximise their profits. He used a sample of seventeen industries and found some relationship between 1953-57 rates of return and 1954 four firms concentration ratios in excess of 80 per cent. He, however, was very cautious to draw any conclusion from his data as he indicated that there was no relationship between profitability and concentration if the share of the four largest firms was less than about 80 per cent.

Mann (1966) used 1950-60 data to study the relation between four digit industry concentration ratios and accounting rates of return. The sample was drawn from 30 four-digit industries where barriers of entry could be estimated. His results were similar to the Bain's findings. He revealed that twenty-one industries with more than 70 per cent eight-firm concentration ratios earned an average return or 13.3 per cent while the nine industries having less than 70 per cent concentration showed an average return of 9.0 per cent. He attributed the differences in profitability of industries to entry barriers.

Shepherd (1972) conducted a company based cross-section study on structure and profitability relationship in large US firms for 1960-69. He formed a sample of 231 firms and also made certain subsets within these 231 firms. The subsets were made for 'young industry firms', 'old industry firms', 'consumer goods firms', and 'producer goods firms'. For 179 firms the data were available for the period 1965-69 and he reported their results as well. The variables included in the study were: market share, size, advertising to sales ratio, four-firm concentration ratio, rest of group (computed by deducting market share from concentration ratio) and revenue growth. The market share was found positively and strongly related consistently in all the equations. The size showed negative co-efficient throughout. The coefficient of advertising intensity was positive and significant in all the equations except for 'consumer goods firms'. The growth was also positive and significant. To sum up, market share turned out to be the main element of market structure.

Gale (1972) examined a sample of 106 firms for 1963-67 operating in four-digit standard industrial classification industries to investigate the impact of market share on profitability. The influence of growth on profits was also examined. The findings indicated that high market share led to superior performance and the impact of market share on performance depended on firm and industry features. The share-profitability relationship was stronger in large firms operating in highly concentrated industries growing at moderate rate. The relationship between profitability and risk was positive and significant. As per expectation, leverage, firm growth as well as industry growth bore positive signs and were significant in all the equations. The effect of concentration on profit was positive and significant for high concentration industries and it was non-significant for medium concentration industries.

Based on a sample of 241 four-digit manufacturing industries from the 1963 Census of Manufactures, Rhoades (1973) conducted a study to examine the relationship between industry profitability and diversification. Apart from diversification variables, concentration, growth in demand, capital output ratio were employed as control variables in the industry structure-framework to examine the impact of diversification on profit performance. All the regression equations produced expected results in respect of concentration, growth and capital output ratio by revealing positive and significant coefficients. However, in respect of one of the two diversification variables, the results were contrary to expectations. One diversification variable demonstrated a systematic relationship with industry profitability and this relationship was linked to barriers to entry. On the other hand, the other diversification variable appeared to be a measure of the ease of entry.

To study the association between competition and profitability, McEnally (1976) formed two groups of industries to represent the degree of competitiveness. He could do this for only 16 industries comprising 179 companies over the period 1950-65. The two groups of industries he formed were—'very high barriers to entry industries' and 'other barriers to entry industries'. The first category represented monopolistic while the second competitive industries. The results of the study indicated categorically that competition lowered profitability differentials among industries. The monopolistic industries earned higher profits. Moreover, industries with higher average return tended to have larger variations in inter-firm rates of return.

Dalton and Penn (1976) empirically examined the concentration-profitability relationship. He used a sample of 97 large food-manufacturing firms. He assumed the profitability as function of product differentiation, industry growth, absolute firm size, market share and concentration. The empirical results of the study indicated that there was a critical level of concentration. The profit rates were found to be higher when four-firm concentration was at or above 45 per cent and when eight-firm concentration was at or above 60 per cent. The coefficient of market share variable was positive and significant in both the groups of concentration. This indicated that higher market share might lead to higher profit rates. Advertising was also found positive and significant in the high concentration group. However, the relationship between size and profitability was positive and significant in the low concentration group. This last finding had been stated to be puzzling.

Meehan and Duchesneau (1973) focused their study to examine whether the association between concentration and profitability was discontinuous at some critical level. Their sample consisted of 186 firms classified into 32 four-digit industries. They reported that the relationship between concentration and profitability was discontinuous at a specific critical level. The critical level was found to exist at 55 per cent at four-firm level and 70 per cent at the eight-firm level. The findings suggested that when concentration had reached the critical level it ceased to raise profitability.

Levy (1984) conducted a study to examine if the profit-concentration relationship is homogeneous over industries. He employed a standard market structure-performance model with entry barriers to analyse the data for the years—1963, 1967 and 1972 for a sample of 197 industries. The study rejected the null hypothesis that the concentration-profit relation was homogeneous across industries. His results suggested that the effect of concentration on profit varied substantially in different industries.. He indicated that past studies which had assumed the relationship between concentration and profitability to be homogeneous across industries, might be biased.

Capon *et al.* (1988) carried out a study based on the market structure variables. They related the superior performance to the specialisation by market type. Different types of markets required different type of skills for success. Therefore, firms should concentrate by market type and would lead to superior performance, they suggested.

Coate and Uri (1988) examined the relationship between industry structure and economic performance *via* equation model of profitability, concentration, advertising expenditure and research and development expenditure. They used data pertaining to 285 four-digit Standard Industrial Classification (SIC) industries. Apart from the full data sample, they also analysed a subset of data to see if the estimation results were different when a subset sample was used. Advertising intensities were found significantly higher in consumer goods industries. Profitability as well as concentration was also found to be positively related to higher advertising levels. However, concentration did not tend to increase advertising efforts across industries. The analysis of research and development equation revealed that concentration and imports tended to exert higher positive effects on research and development activities. Profits also had positive relationship with research and development outlays. The estimation results of concentration ratio revealed that advertising exerted positive effects on concentration, while research and development outlays had a very slight effect on concentration. Efficiency variable showed strong influence on concentration. The profitability equation revealed that efficiency and import variables were statistically significant and research and development expenditure also had positive correlation with profitability. Advertising tended to exert negative influence on profits, while concentration and growth had positive but insignificant association with profitability. Importantly, when the estimation results of the truncated sample were compared with those of the full data sample, it was found that the impact of concentration on advertising expenditure became statistically significant in truncated sample from statistically insignificant in the full sample. Moreover, the effect of profitability variable on advertising was statistically more strong in the truncated sample. Equally, the results were also sensitive to the data sample used for the research and development expenditure equation. However, the results of the concentration equation and the profitability equation experienced few changes over the two samples. Hence, they empirically showed that different data sets might lead to different conclusions and it might be the cause of disagreement among the researchers.

Coate (1989) examined the intertemporal behaviour of profitability in oligopoly industries. His sample included 48 highly concentrated 4-digit industries. He classified the data into consumer goods and producer goods industries. He also subdivided the sample into increasing, constant and decreasing concentration industries. The results of the study suggested that above normal profits would rather disappear when persist over time. Concentration tended to increase profit in few industries. Concentration effect was found only in those industries where concentration was changing, i.e. it was increasing or decreasing. Moreover, concentration effect was more in consumer goods industries.

Schmalensee's (1985) study is the first cross-section study which aimed squarely at the decomposition of profitability variation into various effects. He used data of 456 large multi-divisional firms in 242 FTC manufacturing industries for 1975 and decomposed the profitability variation into industry, corporate, and market share components. His results revealed neither the existence of firm effects nor the importance of market share effects. Moreover, industry effects were found to be the strongest and accounted for about 75 per cent of the variance of industry performance differential.

Scott and Pascoe (1986), using the Federal Trade Commission's (FTC's) Line of Business (LB) data, found firm and industry effects to be significant. The industry characterising variables they used were— concentration, minimum efficient scale, import competition, geographic size of the market served by the industry, growth of market demand and cost of capital appropriate for an industry. Firm specific variables used by them were— diversification and leverage. Three variables that provided neither firm-wide nor industry-wide characteristics, were—each company's average share of the particular industry, advertising to sales ratio and ratio of assets to sales. While concluding their paper they pointed emphatically that important effects were not captured by firm-wide or industry-wide variables independently of one another.

Kessides (1990), using data of 456 large multi-divisional firms operating in 242 FTC manufacturing industries for 1975, conducted a study to disintegrate variation in firm profitability across industries into firm, industry and market share effects. He reported the existence of firm, industry and market share effects. He showed that all of these were both statistically significant and quantitatively important and accounted for a major portion of dispersion of rates of return.

Amato and Wilder (1990) conducted a comprehensive cross-section study using data for the years 1966 and 1975 with a sample of 40 manufacturing industries. They included risk, elasticity, business cycle effects, firm size, market share, concentration, advertising intensity, minimum efficient scale, import ratio and capital intensity in the model. They captured the industry effects by employing industry dummy variables and found industry effects to be significant in explaining cross-sectional variation in profitability. Their findings were consistent with Schmalensee (1985) and Scott and Pascoe (1986).

Rumelt* (1991) broke up the total variance in profitability among FTC Line of Business into industry factors, time factors, factors associated with the corporate parent and business specific factors. He held a *post mortem* examination of Schmalensee's 1985 sample consisting of 1975 LB data of FTC. To correct the weakness, instead of a single year data he analysed the FTC LB data of four years from 1974 to 1977. Moreover, he split the overall business cycle effects into stable and transient industry effects as well as stable and transient business unit effects. Like Schmalensee, he exhibited negligible corporate effects but surprisingly his findings revealed small stable industry effects and very large business unit effects. He showed that stable industry effects accounted for only 8 per cent of the variance in business returns. Furthermore, only about 40 per cent of the dispersion in industry returns was due to stable industry effects. Precisely, industry membership was found much less important.

The empirical evidences of the positive correlation between high concentration and profitability have led the economists to relate the high concentration with monopoly power and collusive

---

* Rumelt can be related more to strategic management research. Within strategic management there is growing group who cross over between the fields. Rumelt is one of them.

practices. A great number of studies on this subject have revealed that persistent concentration may have unfavourable effect on output and price. Such evidences have been the bases to formulate public policy towards business. In India MRTP Act, 1969 had been enacted to reduce concentration of economic power in few hands. The industry, in which a few firms' market share was very high, was named as 'oligopoly industry' and any firm having high market share was designated as 'oligopoly firm'. Such firms were then subjected to the Act for deconcentration.

Brozen (1970), however, had some suspicion on the empirical relationship between concentration and profitability that had been investigated by a substantial number of studies and supported by most of them. He argued that if firms operating in highly concentrated industries earned high rates of return by virtue of some successful collusion, such high rates of return should have persisted over time.

Brozen reacted to a proposal draft of a Concentrated Industries Act to reduce concentration. The Act was guided by the assumption that the relationship between rates of return and concentration ratio had a link with collusive practices. He studied the samples of Bain, Mann and Stigler by extending them beyond their original time frame to investigate if the high rates of return in highly concentrated industries reported by these studies persisted over time. His examination revealed that high rates of return in highly concentrated industries did not persist over time. Hence, Brozen suggested that market itself would do the work of deconcentration and reduce the monopoly profit over time.

Demsetz (1973) empirically showed that there existed a positive relationship between profitability and industrial concentration. He based his study on the 1963 rate of return partitioned into 4 size classes of firms and 6 levels of industry concentration for 95 three-digit industries. He found that large firms operating in highly concentrated industries earned higher rates of return than that of the smaller firms. Nevertheless, he explained this relationship from a different perspective. He argued that larger firms operating in highly concentrated industries might have been earning higher rate of return by virtue of their competitive superiority and not due to collusive practices. He observed that deconcentration policies made to eliminate inefficiency might rather produce more inefficiency. Moreover, examination of small firms in concentrated industries *vis-à-vis* small firms in competitive industries revealed that the former were not more profitable. To be brief, his study indicated that increased profitability in high concentrated industries was due to the superior efficiency of large firms.

Peltzman (1977) studied a sample of 165 four-digit Standard Industrial Classification (SIC) manufacturing industries over the period 1947-67 to investigate the concentration-profitability relationship. He found a positive relationship between the two, but concentration-profitability was not related solely to collusion. Efficiency effects were reported to dominate. The findings indicated that higher concentration reduced costs. An inverse relationship was identified between changes in concentration and changes in costs. In other words, the higher the concentration, the more the reduction in costs.

Carter (1978) empirically analysed the data for the years 1963, 1967 and 1972 to find out whether the positive and significant relationship between concentration and profitability was due to collusion between leading firms. Two samples were formed for each of the three years. The first sample consisted of all the manufacturing industries for which the requisite data were available. The second sample was formed by dropping all the n.e.c. (not elsewhere classified) and miscellaneous industries. Then two size classes were constructed for both the samples. The first size class termed as 'leading firms' included the top four firms in an industry. The second size class termed as 'secondary firms' consisted of the next four largest firms. The results of all the equations revealed that concentration coefficients for profitability were positive and significant for only the leading firms in both the samples. However, the coefficients of advertising intensity and capital intensity variables were found to be positive and significant in all the equations for leading as well as secondary firms. Thus, concentration ratios were found associated with higher profits of large firms only. To conclude, the study strongly supported Demsetz's conclusion that superior efficiency of large firms underlay the profit-concentration association.

Ravenscraft (1983) investigated the association between profit and concentration at the Line of Business (micro) and industry (macro) level. A number of structural variables were included in the model to analyse the relationship. The sample consisted of data on 3,186 LB operating in 285 four-digit FTC manufacturing industries for the year 1975. The regression results of industry equation were considerably different from those of the LB equation. Industry advertising was found positively associated with profitability. However, in LB equation advertising had negative impact on profitability. Industry equation indicated that large firms enjoyed comparatively higher returns than their smaller counterparts. This finding had been reported to be akin to that of Demsetz (1973). In other words, increased profitability in highly concentrated industries was supposed to be due to the superior efficiency of large firms. The results of the LB regression, on the other hand, depicted concentration impact on profitability to be negative.

Bothwell, Cooley and Hall (1984) used a sample of 156 large US manufacturing firms over the period 1960-67 to analyse the relationship between market structure and performance. They tested six hypotheses which were developed from the past empirical researches in the field of industrial organisation. No support was found for collusion hypothesis which assumed that high concentration and high profits are related due to monopoly power. Equally, the hypotheses of barriers to entry, the absolute firm size and the 'risk premium' did not find any convincing support. However, the advertising hypothesis as well as the relative firm size hypothesis got the strongest support. A positive correlation was also reported between growth and profitability.

Chappell and Cottle (1985) investigated the concentration-profitability relationship to find the relative role of efficiency and collusion in explaining the industry profitability. Their sample contained 274 four-digit manufacturing industries. However, data on all the variables were available in respect of only 263 industries. Two different industry profit equations were employed to analyse the data for different firm sizes in each industry. In the first equation concentration was the main explanatory variable and in the second both concentration and efficiency variables were assumed to explain the profitability. The regression results of the first equation revealed that concentration exerted positive and significant influence on profitability in the larger size classes. However, the coefficient was negative and insignificant for the smaller size classes. This finding was akin to that of Demsetz's and indicated that larger firms earned profits higher than those of smaller firms by virtue of their higher efficiency. The results of the second equation in which both concentration and three efficiency variables were included as explanatory variables, revealed that concentration was positive but insignificant for the largest size class and negative but insignificant for the rest of the three size classes. They concluded that when concentration was included in the profitability equation without the efficiency variables, it was simply reflecting the effects of efficiency variables.

Studies in Other Countries

Orr (1974) analysed the cross-section differences in entry between 71 three-digit Canadian manufacturing industries. High concentration, advertising intensity and capital requirements were found to be significant barriers to entry. Industry size exerted positive influence on entry while R & D intensity and risk turned out to be of moderate importance. Barriers to entry allowed higher profits and induced fewer entrants. Advertising was found to be highly and positively correlated with profitability in the consumer goods industries. In another similar paper, Orr (1974a) examined the role of entry barriers in the market structure-performance relationship. He constructed an index of the overall level of entry barriers form each 71 three-digit Canadian manufacturing industries. The entry barriers which they included in the study were capital requirements, advertising intensity, R&D, risk and high concentration. For the sake of comparison with Mann (1966), the total sample was divided into three categories with respect to the index of entry barriers, viz. highest, average and lowest. Like Bain (1956) and Mann (1966) it was found that high barrier industries enjoyed significantly higher profits but low barrier industries were not significantly less profitable than others. Moreover, highly concentrated industries with highest barriers were found to be more profitable. Again, this finding was consistent with that of Bain and Mann.

Neumann, Bobel, and Haid (1979) examined the relationship between profitability, risk and market structure in West German industries. They utilised data on 334 companies assigned to their respective 3-digit industry groups over the period 1965-73. The average rates of return of the bigger firms were consistently higher than those of the smaller firms on all the four measures of profitability. The results suggested that risk and market structure variables substantially explained the profitability of German companies. The relationship of risk, concentration, product differentiation and growth with profitability was positive and significant.

Cubbin and Geroski (1987) conducted a study with a sample of 217 large UK firms over the period 1951-77. Firms were allocated among 48 three-digit industries. Their major concern was to find how important firm and industry effects were in explaining movements in profitability over time. They developed various models to decompose firm profits into firm and industry specific factors. They reported the existence of industry effects and revealed that most of the variations were due to industry characteristics mainly industry concentration.

Masuda (1993) analysed the competitivity of the Japanese highly concentrated industries. He utilised the data on 54 companies operating in 20 industries. The 20 industries were grouped into high and low concentrated industries. The two period of analysis were 1971-77 and 1978-85. He found that highly concentrated industries were generally subjected to competitive pressure and high profit rates in the highly concentrated industries would move toward the long run equilibrium.

Studies in Developing Countries

Most of the research work relating to inter-industry performance differences has been undertaken in industrially advanced countries and particularly in USA. A few studies conducted in less developed countries (LDCs) are reviewed in this section.

White (1974) examined the relationship between concentration and profitability using data of the firms listed on the Karachi Stock Exchange in Pakistan for 1964 and 1965. The sample was restricted to 17 industries. He found a positive and significant relationship between rate of returns and concentration. The capacity utilisation variable in his study was not significant at all. He himself indicated that his results were not wholly satisfactory as the sample was small.

Sharwani (1976) carried out a firm based study of relationship between concentration and profitability. He used data for four years ending 1967, 1968, 1970 and 1973. His sample comprised of 283 large firms operating in Pakistan's 27 large manufacturing industries. Two indicators of profits were used, namely pre-tax profit as a percentage of paid-up capital and pre-tax profit as a percentage of paid-up capital and reserves. The coefficients of concentration variables were positive and significant for both the indicators of profitability.

Amjad (1977) studied the impact of concentration on profitability for the years between 1965 and 1970. His sample consisted of 25 industries operating in the large scale manufacturing sector in West Pakistan. Price-cost margin was used as the indicator of profitability. The concentration showed up an important factor in explaining inter-industry profitability variations. The capital intensity variable was not significantly associated with profitability while the coefficient of capacity utilisation was positive and significant in all the regression equations except for the year 1967-68.

Gan and Tham (1977) tested the relationship between market structure and economic performance with Malaysians data. His sample contained 42 four-digit manufacturing industries. Price-cost margin averaged for the period 1968-71 was taken as the dependant variable. The independent variables employed in the multiple regression equation were: 8-firm concentration ratio, export output ratio, effective tariff protection, direct foreign investment, growth of market demand and capital output ratio. Minimum efficient scale, absolute capital requirement, and advertising to sales ratio were employed as three types of entry barriers. The coefficient of seller concentration ratios was positive in all the equations, but it was significant at only 10 per cent level in the equation in which variables of absolute capital requirement and direct foreign investment were excluded. The non-significance of the concentration ratio had been stated to be the attribute of multi-collinearity among certain independent variables. All other variables had positive and significant impact on PCM except direct foreign investment variables which were not significant and export output ratio which had negative relationship with Price-Cost Margin (PCM). The analysis was also made for two separate subsets of consumer goods industries and producer goods industries. The coefficient of seller concentration variable was again not significant in both the equations. The coefficient of minimum efficient scale variable and capital output ratio were positive and significant in both the equations while advertising to sales ratio and direct foreign investment variable were positive and significant in only consumer goods industries. All other variables had no significant impact on PCM.

Reekie (1984) examined the state of structure-conduct-performance (SCP) paradigm by using South African data. His sample consisted of 26 three-digit manufacturing industries. He found that the association between concentration and profitability held good in South African industries. The more concentrated half of the sample industries showed higher profitability than the less concentrated half. He concluded that even after neutralising the effect of scale, innovations and market share factors the SCP model was justified although partially.

Jeong and Masson (1990) used Korean data for 1976-81 to test structure-conduct-performance model. The sample was made of 62 manufacturing industries out of which 32 were consumer goods industries and the remainders were producer goods industries. The results suggested that high profits attracted entry and this process caused fall in profits. In the concentration equation, barriers were found positive and significant with the exception of significance of advertising in consumer goods industries. However, the entry was negative and significant while growth and concentration was positively associated. In entry equation, concentration and entry showed positive and significant association. The profit equation revealed the association of concentration with profits and advertising to be positive and significant.

Studies Conducted in India

Gupta (1968) is the pioneer to conduct a study to examine the relationship between structure and performance in India. He tested the hypothesis of positive relationship between profitability, barriers to entry, and concentration ratio on 29 Indian manufacturing industries for 1958. The three indicators of barriers to entry used were: relative market-size of the minimum optimal plant, coefficient of steepness of the average cost curve, and capital requirements for the minimum optimum plant-size. The concentration ratio was defined as the percentage of total industrial employment accounted for by the four largest units in the industry. The profit rate of 1958 was used as an indicator of profitability but its definition was not given. No significant relationship was found between height of barriers to entry, profitability and concentration. However, he refrained from accepting or rejecting the hypothesis of a positive and significant relationship between the rate of return, height of barriers to entry and concentration ratio.

Walgreen (1971) *post martemed* Gupta's (1968) data with a different methodology and unlike him, produced results which were in line with the results produced by Bain and Mann in their studies with US industry data. For the sake of comparability with earlier studies, he arranged Gupta's data according to Bain's classification to test the relationship between scale economies and profitability. Concentration ratios were also rearranged to examine the relationship between concentration and profitability. Both the relationships turned to be positive and significant when alternative methodology was used. He attributed the changes in results to certain elapses in Gupta's study. The chief among them was the use of short run data to test a long run relationship.

Sawhney and Sawhney (1973) carried out a study on inter-industry profitability variations. He used a sample of 25 Indian manufacturing industries. He employed the OLS regression technique and step-wise regression procedure to study the impact of various variables on profit rates. The explanatory variables used were: concentration ratio, capital output ratio, and capacity utilisation. Non-linear relationship between profitability and concentration was also tested. The ratio of price to average variable cost averaged over six years (1953-58) was used as measure of profitability. Besides this, an alternative indicator of profitability was also used to analyse the results, viz. Return on Sales (ROS). Concentration ratio was defined as percentage share of total industrial output accounted for by the largest eight units (in terms of employment) in the industry. The impact of all the variables employed was positive and significant on all the measures of profitability at 5 per cent level except the capital output variable in respect of which the coefficient was not significant.

In one of the few studies on concentration in India, Maharatna (1983) examined the variation of concentration over time as well as the impact of concentration on industrial growth. His sample consisted of 66 industries and it covered the period 1964-80. To study the changes over time, he analysed the data for two sub-periods, 1964-75 and 1975-80. The study was based on only 2-firm and 3-firm production concentration ratios. The study failed to reveal any association between the initial level of concentration and its subsequent change over time. However, the analytical results of the two sub-periods suggested that this relationship was negative in the sub-period 1964-75 during which excessive restrictions and controls were imposed in the Indian manufacturing sector. The relationship was positive for the sub-period 1975-80 which enjoyed rather liberal environment. In other words, this finding suggested that high initial concentration would not exert negative impact on the subsequent rise in concentration in the absence of restrictions and controls. Additionally, a positive but weak association was found between initial concentration and growth performance.

Siddhathan and Dasgupta (1983) conducted study on market structure and profitability. Their sample contained medium and large-scale public limited companies operating in 30 industries for the three-year period 1975-76 to 1977-78. Profit after tax as a percentage of net worth was employed as dependent variable. The independent variables in the regression equation were—growth of sales, advertising expenditure, R&D expenditure, size, skill, exports and concentration. In all the regression equations, export variable had consistently negative coefficients while all other variables were positively related to profitability. Skill variable turned out to be the main determinant of profitability. Concentration had no significant relationship with profitability.

Aggarwal (1992) carried out a study of performance variation across industries. The study was based on 42 large manufacturing industries and the results were taken for 1974-78, 1982-86, and 1973-86. Performance was operationalised in terms of physical, financial and economic indicators. Price-Cost Margins (PCMs) and Return on Capital Employed (ROCE) were employed as indicators of financial performance. The study reported the existence of inter-industry performance differentials. The independent variables employed in the study were—effective protection rates, concentration ratio, export intensity, skill levels, wage rates, scale economies, growth ownership etc. As regarding PCM, concentration and skill levels had positive and significant impact while export intensity was negatively and significantly related. Ownership, growth and protection did not show up significant. For ROCE, concentration and protection were not found significant. Ownership had negative impact in both periods, i.e. 1974-78 and 1982-86. Scale economies were important for only 1970s, while export intensity, skill levels and wage rates had significant impact on ROCE for 1980s only.

3

OBJECTIVES AND METHODOLOGY

This cross-section study of inter-industry performance differentials is based on the investigation of 187 companies operating in 21 industries in the private corporate sector over a period of 11 years. This chapter explains in detail the objectives, period, scope and the sample of the study. It also discusses the variables and statistical techniques used to carry out the objectives of the study.

Objectives of the Study

The major objective of this study is to investigate the performance differences among various industries in India. The specific objectives of the study are as below:

(i) To study the performance differences among various industries *vis-à-vis* their profitability;

(ii) To investigate the inter-industry performance differences in terms of growth;

(iii) To explore the determinants of performance by employing structural and other control variables in multiple regression models.

Period of the Study

The period chosen for the study ranges from 1980-81 to 1990-91. This 11-year period was intentionally chosen because the requisite data for the study was easily available when this study was started. Besides, such span provides sufficient data to capture the overall business cycle effects and is sufficient to produce meaningful results in the light of ever-changing economic conditions and political set up both in and outside the country. The additional advantage of this study span is that it covers the period of two five-year plans, viz. the Sixth Five-Year Plan (1980-85) and the Seventh Five-Year Plan (1985-90) which evidently precede the time when a wave of liberalisation and privatisation started in the country in 1991 and brought out radical charges in the economic scenario of the nation.

Selection of Sample Industries and Sample Companies

To validate a meaningful study, we attempted to make a sample of sufficient number of manufacturing and non-manufacturing industries each consisting a set of 10 largest companies in terms of 11-year sales. The selection of ten largest companies in each industry for which data could be obtained for the period under study was the most difficult task of data collection. Initially we started with the Business Standard, an annual number of *Amrit Bazar Patrika* which publishes the list of top 300 companies ranked on the basis of sales, profits, total assets, capitalisation etc. From some time back it was also providing industry-wise classification of top 300 companies. However, when these companies were grouped under each industry over the study period, we were left with a too small number of companies in some industries to validate a meaningful study. Consequently, we had to give up this source to sort out ten top companies in each industry. However, the list of companies arrived at with the help of the Business Standard guided us immensely to prepare the final list of sample companies.

The Stock Exchange Official Directory (SEOD) has the widest coverage regarding the number of public limited companies. The directory is primarily based on annual reports including balance sheets and profit and loss accounts published by its member companies every year. Moreover, it is the only single source which provides information on the greatest number of items for the highest number of years (10 years) at one place. Furthermore, it also provides an exhaustive list of companies pertaining to different industries. But the industry-wise classification of companies done by it is rather crude; some companies have been classified under more than one industry. Equally, it does not provide categorically the information on the type of ownership of companies.

The Centre for Monitoring Indian Economy (CMIE) publishes key financial data of the larger business units. It also provides information on the type of ownership and industry category of each company covered by it very lucidly and systematically. Hence, SEOD and CMIE proved to be complimentary to finalise the sample for this study. We compiled an exhaustive list of companies pertaining to different industries from SEOD and cross-checked every company with CMIE to sort out the 10-top companies based on 11 years' average sales in each industry to make up the sample for this study. The comprehensive list of companies from SEOD was modified by deleting the firms:

- — which were not in operation for any year during the period under study;
- — which were in operation but for which the financial data were not available for any of the 11-year period under study;
- — which were not operating in the private corporate sector throughout the period under study;
- — which were diversified and could not be assigned to any specific industry.
- — companies which derived less than 50 per cent of its gross sales from one of the products of an industry group, were classified as diversified companies. This study has been carried out for three different classification of industry. The make-up of samples for the three classifications of industries is contained in Table 3.1.

Industry-wise Classification of Companies

Though there are a number of different classification systems of industries, there is as yet no one unanimously accepted industry classification suitable for all purposes. The concept of an industry has become blurred because firms have diversified their activities into related as well as unrelated areas. Researchers have shown that diversification has been continuously increasing. Firms are moving into new industries as the primary markets have become

Table 3.1 : Make up of Samples for Different Industry Classification Systems

Industry Group	Number of Companies
Commodity/Activity Based Classification	
1. Aluminium	06
2. Automobile	10
3. Cement	10
4. Cotton Textile	10
5. Electrical Machinery	09
6. Fertiliser	06
7. Iron and Steel	10
8. Jute	08
9. Man-made Fibre	14
10. Paint	06
11. Paper	10
12. Pharmaceuticals	10
13. Sugar	10
14. Tea	10
15. Tobacco	04
16. Tyre and Tube	10
17. Vanaspati	04
18. Construction	09
19. Electricity	07
20. Shipping	09
21. Trading	10
Total	172
Use Based Classification	
1. Basic Goods	40
2. Intermediate Goods	42
3. Capital Goods	16
4. Consumer Goods	61
Total	159
Input Based Classification	
1. Agro-based	56
2. Metal-based	23
3. Chemical-based	36
'otal	115

saturated. Now most of the companies are operating in various industries and there are few companies which are operating in only one industry.

In this study, industry-wise groupings have been done on the basis of National Industrial Classification (NIC) of all economic activities (taken up by the companies). Under the NIC system all the factories are classified in their appropriate industry group on the basis of the value of principal product manufactured by them. In this way a unit gets classified exclusively in one industry group even though it might be manufacturing products belonging to different industries. NIC, besides being the most comprehensive survey of industry, is also comparable to the International Standard Industrial Classification (ISIC), the classification used internationally. Moreover a large number of earlier studies have also made use of this classification and the results of this study could be comparable with them [e.g. Siddharthan and Dasgupta (1983); Aggarwal (1992)]. CMIE is also following this system of classification. CMIE classifies a company under a particular industry group if more than half of its gross sales are derived from one of the products of that industry group. Companies which cannot be classified in any of the industries in this manner, are classified as diversified companies. In this study, the CMIE's publication *Key Financial Data on Larger Business Units,* January 1993 issue, was consulted to classify the companies into different industries. However, if this information was not available for some companies in this issue of CMIE due to non-coverage, the same was collected from its earlier issues.

As mentioned earlier, industries are difficult to define and in many cases depend upon past custom and practice. While industries and markets may coincide, but it is not necessary that they always do so. For example, scooters, motorcycles, cars, and trucks are all part of the automobile industry, yet each competes in a different market. Though efforts have been made to do the Commodity/Activity-based classification in a way that industries and markets may coincide, it was not possible in case of some products/activities due to wide variety of products and lack of sufficient number of companies in each product group, namely electrical machinery, man-made fibre, iron and steel etc. Due care has been taken to consider this factor when a variable of industry level is introduced in the analysis. For example, in analysing the relationship between market structure and performance, concentration ratios have been constructed in such a way that each company is assigned the concentration ratio of only that product group in which it competes, e.g. in automobile industry, companies producing heavy commercial vehicles and two wheelers have been assigned concentration ratios of their respective product groups.

Apart from Commodity/Activity-based classification of industry, the study has also been carried out for two other economically meaningful groupings of industries, viz. Use-based and Input-based classification of industries. These two classification systems are basically extracted from the NIC and the both are widely used by policy makers and researchers (see Ahluwalia, 1985; Kaur, 1992). The Input-based classification is also used by Economic Survey (Ministry of Finance); Report on Currency and Finance (published by Department of Economic Analysis and Policy for Reserve Bank of India, Bombay).

Scope of the Study

This study has been confined to private sector only. The public sector enterprises are different from the ones operating in private sector and it is very difficult to compare the performance of private sector enterprises with those of the public sector. This issue has been taken up subsequently.

The Mixed Economy : Public Sector vs. Private Sector

At the time of independence, almost the entire economy was in the hands of private sector. Soon after independence, the Industrial Policy Resolution of 1948 marked the dawn of mixed economy in India and both, public as well as private sector began to operate. Although the share of the public sector in Indian economy increased tremendously, the private sector continued to play an important and dominant role. This is evident from Tables 3.2 and

3.3 below :

Table 3.2 : Percentage Share of Public and Private Sectors in NDP

(at current prices)

Year	1950-51	1960-61	1970-71	1990-91
Public Sector	7.5	10.6	14.5	23.8
Private Sector	92.5	89.4	85.5	76.2

Source: Central Statistical Organisation, National Accounts Statistics, 1970-71, 1984-85, January, 1987,1993.

Table 3.3 : Growth of the Private Corporate Sector in India

(in terms of number of companies)

Year	March 1957	March 1971	March 1991
No. of companies	29,357 (100)	30,461 (100)	2,20,721 (100)
(a) Government	74 (0.25)	314 (1.03)	1179 (0.53)
(b) Non-Government	29,283 (99.75)	30,147 (98.97)	2,19,542 (99.47)

Note: Figures in brackets are percentages of total.
Source: CMIE, Basic Statistics relating to the Indian Economy, August 1992.

Table 3.2 shows that the share of the public sector has increased significantly in NDP. Nevertheless, the private sector occupies a dominant position in the economy. As private sector is generally equated with the private corporate sector in a narrow sense, Table 3.3 shows the growth of the private corporate sector *vis-à-vis* the growth of the public sector (in terms of number of companies). To sum up, notwithstanding the emphasis on public sector in the past, private sector continued to be dominant.

All Western economies have been mixed economies for many years and there has been a debate concerning the role of public and private sector. Millward (1982) sought to compare the performance of public and private enterprises. He observed that it was not easy to compare the performance of private sector enterprise with that of public sector enterprise. He pointed out that a comparison made on the basis of relative profitability might produce different results. He cited the cases in evidence drawn from UK, USA, Canada, Australia and Switzerland. In India too, this fact has been highlighted from time to time at various places. Late Jawaharlal Nehru had envisaged that the role of public sector was to be instrumental to the growth and development of the country and to contribute to build such a sound economic base in which the private sector might flourish. Moreover, the performance criteria for public enterprises cannot be the same as those for private enterprises for several reasons. Firstly, unlike private enterprises, they have an instrumental role and this may imply carrying out of policies such as providing equal opportunity for employment, location in depressed areas, welfare of employees, good corporate citizenship, exports even if unprofitable, and the like. Such obligatory costs may not always be born by any comparable private sector unit. Secondly, quite often there are no comparable enterprise in terms of size, structure, technology and product mix in the domestic private sector. Thirdly, the rationale for having these enterprises in the public sector, *inter alia*, the lack of experience in the country with regard to the management of new complex enterprises based on sophisticated technology. It may, therefore, be unfair to compare the profitability of public sector units with those of private sector units providing similar product lines.

Apart from this, public sector undertakings usually enjoy special privileges, e.g. the erstwhile Monopolies and Restrictive Trade Practices Act, 1969 (MRTP Act, 1969) did not apply to public sector units on the ground that such units were established for the furtherance of state policies for public good and were quite often meant to be a remedial measure to prevent the concentration of economic power in private hands. All the more, this act sought to promote competition among private enterprises, *per se*, at various levels of production and the distribution of goods and services by controlling monopolistic and restrictive trade practices.

The perusal of industrial policy resolutions, five year plan documents and other official statements, reveals that the objectives of public enterprises in India have been to promote economic development, growth, self-reliance, research and development, innovative management practices and to generate employment adequate return on investment etc. Besides and this; the public sector has to fulfil certain socio-economic objectives. For instance, sometimes public enterprises subsidise the prices of goods and services which are generally consumed by the poorer sections of the society. Hence, it is evident from the preceding discussion chart, unlike the private sector, the maximisation of profit has not been the principle concern of public sector, instead the public sector the public sector has to primarily shoulder the responsibility of the welfare of the country. In the light of the above stated differences between the two sectors, the sample was confined to the private corporate sector only.

The Variables

Measurement of Performance

Performance is an ambiguous phenomenon and it can be measured and interpreted in a variety of different ways. Performance simply reflects the degree of success achieved in terms of stated objectives and as the objectives differ widely so does the concept of performance. Performance can be viewed differently from different perspectives. An economic planner is particular about the efficient utilisation of resources while a welfare economist would also be concerned with the equitable distribution of gains apart from efficient utilisation of resources. From the national viewpoint, performance indicators would consist of overall socio-economic development, generation of employment, promotion of research and development, upgradation of technology, training, education and health facilities etc. Moreover, performance may connote different meanings according to the different level of economic development. Furthermore, there are different parties interested in an enterprise and the behaviour of an enterprise, whether private or public, is a reflection of the behaviour of many groups, viz. management, labour, owners, consumers, government etc.

Berle and Means (1932) observed that there is a separation between ownership and management in large companies and in such companies, different interested parties view company performance from different viewpoints. Penrose (1959) has rightly remarked that owners are interested in profitability, while managers are interested in growth of the firm. So, a company's performance should be measured in such a way as to incorporate both the dimensions, viz. profitability and growth. In the light of the objectives of this study it would be quite reasonable to use a measure that can incorporate profitability and growth dimensions of performance. Moreover, we have reasons to expect that growth and profitability are closely related to each other. A firm's rate of growth normally depends on its 'ability' and 'willingness to grow'. The higher the profitability, higher will be its capacity to reinvest, brighter the prospects for new issues in the capital market and higher the ability to grow. Moreover, if management is to feel adequately secure and be reasonably fair to shareholders there has to be a close relation between rate of return and maximum sustainable growth.

Choice of Performance Variables

For the purpose of this study, growth and profitability have been used as the indicators of performance. In the regression models these are used as dependent variables. The following five variables were chosen to measure the performance:

Return on Equity (ROE)
Return on Assets (ROA)
Growth of Sales (GSALES)
Growth in Dividend (GDIV)
Growth in Total Net Assets (GTNA).

ROE and ROA are the indicators of profitability while GSALES, GDIV and GTNA are representatives of growth. ROE reflects the firm's success from the common shareholders' point of view in terms of returns provided to them. It is the most widely used profitability measure. ROA serves as the measure of management's efficiency and effectiveness in utilising all the assets under its control. Moreover, it is not effected by the difference in the capital structure of the firm. Like ROE, it is also a widely used indicator of profitability. GSALES represents the firm's success in its markets. GDIV reflects the short-term return on investment by the equity holders. GTNA is a general growth indicator. In the study, we have computed 11-year averages of each measure and then converted this to an annual equivalent rate. This long-term approach to measure performance is considered necessary to reduce short-term fluctuations in performance variables.

Computation of Performance Variables

The ROE and ROA have been computed by employing the following formulae:

$$\text{ROE} = \frac{\text{Earnings after interest, tax \& preference dividend}}{\text{Shareholders' funds}}$$

$$\text{ROA} = \frac{\text{Earnings before interest, tax and all dividends}}{\text{Total assets}}$$

The compound growth rate of sales, dividend and total net assets over the period 1980-81 to 1990-91 have been computed with the help of following model:

$Y = a + bt + e$
y = Value of variable
a = Intercept
b = Slope
t = Time variable
e = Error term

The formula to compute the compound rate 'r' is :

$$r = (\text{antilog } b - 1) \times 100$$

Where b is the Ordinary Least Square estimator of b in the regression model given above.

Sales means net sales or total revenue derived by deducting goods returned, allowances and discounts from the gross amount received from sales. Dividend is the total dividend (interim *plus* final) paid to the equity shareholders during the year. Total net assets are total assets less current and long-term liabilities and intangible assets.

Explanatory Variables

There is multiplicity of factors which may be responsible for differences in the performance of firms. It is, therefore, necessary to control the impact of such factors on performance. The followings have been used as the explanatory variables in the regression models in order to disintegrate their impact on performance.

Industry Membership
Leverage
Capital Intensity
Age
Risk
Skill
Size
Concentration Ratios
Capacity Utilisation
Market Share

Industry membership is a non-metric variable while all other variables are metric variables. Industry membership has been employed as the dummy variable representing 21 industries (or so depending upon the type of industry classification) useds in various regression models. Computation of these variables is provided in the respective chapters of their use. We also tried to include in this study imports, exports, research and development expenditure and advertising intensity variables in addition to the aforesaid control variables, but data on these variables were beyond our reach—since it involved hefty cost (reasons detailed in the next section). Hence, we have to drop these variables.

Collection of Data

After defining the sample list of industries and finalising the list of companies in each industry for this study, the next task was to collect the required data in the light of objectives of the research. The data have been collected from the secondary sources only, mainly from the various issues of the Stock Exchange Official Directory (SEOD) and the Centre for Monitoring Indian Economy (CMIE). The SEOD is the only single source which provides the widest coverage at one place in respect of number of items, companies and years. However, it does not provide data on imports, exports, research and development expenditure and advertising expenditure of the companies. Equally, it does not provide product-wise sales break up of companies. We tried to gather the same from the annual reports of the companies under study, which were available in the Research and Statistics Division of the Department of Company Affairs, but as the charges for one year's annual report of one company was rupees ten, we could not afford the same. Although the data on exports and imports were available in the CMIE's publication *Key Financial Data on Larger Business Units*, yet the same were available from the year 1987 onwards and that too in respect of the bigger companies only. This very publication has also started publishing sales break up information on different products of the companies, but, again it was available only after the period under study. Eventually, we have to give up the idea of using the variables which needed information on imports, exports, R&D expenditure, advertising expenditure and product-wise sales break up of companies.

Annualisation of Data

Over the period under study, majority of the sample companies had changed their accounting periods. This made the data of two consecutive years incomparable as the data were not for the same length of time. Mostly the data for a particular year were partially spread over the preceding and/or the following year(s). This would have affected specially the compound growth rates and coefficients of variation of EPS as they were to be computed taking into consideration annual data. To solve this problem, the data were annualised where the accounting year was not of 12 months' duration. Moreover, where the data were missing for a particular year due to change in accounting period, the same were interpolated to make number of observations eleven for the purpose of computing compound growth rates and coefficients of variation of EPS as well.

Statistical Techniques Used

To carry out the objectives of this study, the following statistical techniques have been used. All the statistical work has been done on SPSS/PC+ software.

ANOVA

One Way Analysis of Variance (ANOVA) has been worked out to investigate the performance differentials among various industry groupings. The calculations made utilising the ANOVA procedure generate an F-ratio. The F-ratio is the ratio of the *variance between groups to the variance within groups*. To compute F-ratio we must estimate these two variances. In the process of obtaining an estimate of these two variances, we first calculate a statistic called the *sum of squares* (SS) for each source of variance. From the variance, we calculate the *mean square* (MS) by dividing the sum of squares by the appropriate *degree of freedom* (df). Degree of freedom for the between groups variance are the number of groups minus one, while the degree of freedom for the within groups variance are the total number of subjects minus the number of groups.

Although the ANOVA test enables us to find the strength of significance of inter-industry differentials within the different groups of the industry classification, but we do not know where exactly the differences lie between groups. In order to find out which group means are reliably different, we need one more analysis. The analysis is a multiple comparison test. A multiple comparison test is a test that enables us to compare any and all mean differences in terms of their reliability. The most useful test for making comparison is the Tukey's Test

Tukey's Test

The Tukey test is a useful statistic for comparing each group to every other group (pairwise) to determine which group means are significantly different from each other. The test involves the calculation of a range of statistic (i.e., HSD: Honestly Significant Difference) for each rank that separates one mean from the next. If the differences between these means are larger than the range statistic, the means are reliably different from each other. The computation formula for HSD is given as under:

$$HSD = q(a, df) \sqrt{MS_{error}/n}$$

where $q(a, df)$ = a range statistic for the actual significance level of the F value, and
df = the degree of freedom for the MS_{error}

In this study, inter-industry performance differentials have been studied across five performance variables. Almost all studies show inconsistent results across all the five indicators of performance. It is, therefore, rather a formidable task to say with confidence as to which industry is the best performing. In order to have a Synthetic view of our performance analysis, the information on five performance variables has been condensed by constructing a composite index of performance by using the technique of Factor Analysis.

Factor Analysis

Factor analysis is a statistical technique which can be utilised to examine the underlying patterns or relationships for a large number of variables and determine if the information can be condensed or summarised in a smaller set of factors or components with a minimum loss of information. Factor analysis starts with the calculations of correlation matrix between the variables that are to be summarised. The next step is to construct factor model. The two most commonly employed factor analytic approaches are component analysis and common factor analysis. The component model is used when the objective is to summarise most of the original information in a minimum number of factors for the prediction purposes. In contrast, common factor analysis is used primarily to identify underlying factors not easily recognised. We have used the former approach in the light of our objective. In addition to selecting factor model, the analyst must specify how the factors are to be extracted. Two options are available: orthogonal factors and oblique factors. In the orthogonal solutions, the factors are extracted in such a way so that the factor axes are maintained at 90°, meaning that each factor is independent of all other factors. Therefore, the correlation between factors is arbitrarily determined to be zero. An oblique factor solution is more complex than an orthogonal one. We have used orthogonal solution because an entirely satisfactory analytic procedure has not been devised for oblique solution. Moreover, when the researcher wants to reduce a larger number of variables to a smaller set of uncorrelated variables for subsequent use in regression or other prediction technique, an orthogonal solution is considered the best. There are three major orthogonal approaches: QUARTIMAX, VARIMAX and EQUIMAX. We have used the VARIMAX method because it has proved very successful as an analytic approach to obtain an orthogonal rotation of factors. Moreover, it is most widely utilised. Next, the analyst extracts the initial unrotated factors to explore the data reduction possibilities for a set of variables. However, the final determination of the number of factors is done after the factor matrix is rotated and the factors are interpreted*. The research may stop with factor interpretation but if the extracted factors are to be used for subsequent application to other statistical techniques, the researcher proceeds to the computation of factor scores to create an entirely new set of a smaller number of variables to replace the original set of variables for inclusion in a statistical analysis. In this study, we have computed factor scores to be used as raw data to represent the variables in ANOVA and regression analysis. Finally, we have used Latent root criterion to decide the number of factors to be extracted. As per this criterion, only the factors having latent roots (Eigen values) greater than one are considered significant, all factors with latent roots less than one are considered insignificant and discarded.

The statistical techniques that have been discussed above help us to find whether the inter-industry performance differences are present and also test its statistical significance. But these techniques are not able to decompose the performance variations into various factors. There are number of factors which may be responsible for the performance of firms. We have used multiple regression models in order to disintegrate the impact of such factors on performance.

Multiple Regression Analysis

Multiple regression analysis is a general statistical technique used to analyse the relationship between a single dependent variable and several independent variables. The objective of multiple regression analysis is to use the several independent variables whose values are known to predict the single dependent value the

---

* Unrotated factor solutions extract factors in the order of their importance. The first factor tends to be a general factor with almost every variable loading significantly, and it accounts for the largest amount of variance. The second and subsequent factors are then based upon the residual amount of variance. Rotation of the factors in most cases improves the interpretation by reducing some of the ambiguities that often accompany initial unrotated factor solutions. The ultimate effect of rotating the factor matrix is to redistribute the variance from earlier factors to later ones to achieve a simpler, theoretically more meaningful, factor pattern.

researcher wishes to know. This technique can identify the extent to which each of the independent variables is related to the dependent variable. The following type of multiple regression model of Ordinary Least Square (OLS) has been used in this study to decompose performance variations into various factors:

$$y = \beta_0 + \beta_1 x_1 + \beta_2 x_2 + \ldots\ldots\ldots\ldots + \beta_n x_n + e$$

Where y is the dependent variable; x_1, x_2, ...x_n are the independent variables; β_0 is the intercept. It is the value on the y-axis (dependent variable) where the regression line crosses the axis. It is described as constant term. β_0 is the theoretical estimate of y if x is 0. Moreover, if it is not possible for x to have a value of 0, this result may have no practical interpretation. β_1, β_2 ... β_n are the regression coefficients for respectively the variables x_1, x_2, ...x_n. e is error or residual.

In multiple regression model, (e.g. $y = \beta_0 + \beta_1 x_1 + \beta_2 x_2$), the regression coefficients are partial because each takes into account not only the relationship between y and x_1 and y and x_2 but also the relationship between x_1 and x_2. Moreover when two or more independent variables are measured on different units (e.g., expenditure in rupees, education in years), regression coefficients do not reveal anything about relative importance. To make regression coefficients comparable, the raw data are transformed into new measurement variable with a mean of 0 and standard deviation of 1. When data are transformed in this manner the β_0 term in this regression equation assumes a value of 0. After the data have been standardised, the term *beta coefficient* is often used to denote regression coefficient. We have calculated beta coefficient (standardised regression coefficients) in our statistical analysis.

Seldom will our prediction be perfect. The customary way to assess the adequacy of using the average as a predictor is to examine the errors. Error refers to the difference between the actual number of observations and the estimated number of observations using the arithmetic average as a predictor. By examining the errors, we can know whether the various assumptions underlying the regression analysis are met or not. In this study, the violation of various assumptions has been checked by examining residuals' graphs. Another important aspect of a regression model is to establish how well the model fits. A commonly used measure of the goodness of fit of a linear model is R^2, sometimes called *coefficient of determination*. It measures the proportion of the variation of the dependent variable about its mean that is explained by the independent variable(s). The coefficient may vary between 0 and 1. If the regression model is properly applied and estimated, the higher the value of R^2, the greater the explanatory power of regression equation, and, therefore, the better the prediction of the dependent variable. Note that R^2 is measure of goodness of fit of a particular model and that an R^2 of 0 does not necessarily mean that there is no association between the variables. Instead it indicates that there is no *linear relationship*. In multiple regression analysis, as the number of independent variables in the model increases, so does the R^2. However, this does not necessarily mean that the model with more variables better fits the population. The sample R^2 in general tends to overestimate the population value of R^2. Adjusted R^2 is an attempt to correct the optimistic bias of the sample R^2. *Adjusted* R^2 does not necessarily increase as additional variables are added to an equation. It is the preferred measure of goodness of fit because it is not subject to the inflationary bias of unadjusted R^2. We have interpreted results in this study by calculating *Adjusted* R^2. Finally, to test the appropriateness of regression model, the analysis of variance (ANOVA) can be used, which generates *F-statistics*. The observation of *F-statistics* and its statistical level of significance reveals whether the regression model is appropriate or not.

4

INDUSTRIAL ECONOMICS

Aspects of Performance Differentials

Introduction and Background

This chapter has sought to explain views of industrial economics researchers on performance differentials in industies. These researchers have taken the performance differential aspects from structure and conduct among different industries. Industrialisation plays a key role in the economic development of a country. During the industrialisation process the structure of the economy moves away from agriculture towards manufacturing and services. Most economists consider the development of industry to be essential for economic growth and prosperity of the country. The perusal of Tables 4.1 and 4.2 clearly reveals the adverse relationship between per capita income and agrarian character of the country.

Table 4.1 : Percentage of Active Population Engaged in Agriculture and Industrial Origin of GDP in 1988

Country	Active population engaged in Agriculture*	Industrial origin of GDP percentage distribution		
		Agriculture	Industry	Service
U.K.	3	2	42	56
U.S.A.	4	2	33	65
W. Germany	6	2	51	47
Japan	11	4	45	51
Egypt	46	21	25	54
Pakistan	55	26	24	50
China	74	32	46	21
India	70	32	30	38

* Figures are for 1980

Source: World Bank, *World Development Report*, 1990.

Table 4.2 : Per Capita Income at Market Price

(In US Dollars)

Country	1991
Switzerland	33,610
U.S.A.	22,240
Japan	26,930
Germany	23,650
U.K.	16,500
India	330
China	370

Source: World Bank, *World Development Report*, 1993.

The proportion or population engaged in agriculture in underdeveloped countries is much higher while their per capita income is much less in comparison to developed countries.

Industrialisation process takes place through the activities of a variety of different kinds of business enterprises which operate within markets of varying structural characteristics. A good deal of research work has been undertaken in the field of industrial organisation to study the performance of business enterprises in terms of structural characteristics of their respective markets. Industrial organisation has emerged as a separate field only recently after the rise of modern manufacturing enterprises around the turn of the century. This field is built up more on empirical work and does not have a strong theoretical framework. However, its advancement as a field increasingly depends upon building theory (mainly drawn from economics) that helps in explaining and predicting the conduct and behaviour of firms. Most industrial organisation researchers on business, corporate and industry profitability investigated the causes of differential performance in terms of structural and other variables.

Early work on industrial organisation consisted of case studies of particular industries. However, in 1950s cross-section statistical work on samples of manufacturing industries became popular. Apart from industry as a unit of analysis, industrial organisation also had a strong focus on the firms, and the structure and behaviour of the firms had been the object of study. Hall and Weiss (1967), Shepherd (1972), and others developed the use of company data as the primary unit of analysis. Shepherd (1979) stated that models with company data as the primary unit had grown more adequate and the quality of data improved resulting in estimates with increasing precision.

Structure-Conduct-Performance (SCP) Paradigm

The field of industrial organisation seeks to explain the functioning of enterprises within a variety of market structures. It tries to reveal the forces underlying the structure of markets and its impact on the behaviour and performance of firms in the market. This phenomenon came to be known as structure-conduct-performance (S-C-P) paradigm, in which it is commonly assumed that the performance of business enterprises is strongly influenced by the behaviour and structure of the markets in which they operate.

The S-C-P framework has emerged from the traditional theory of firm in which different types of market structures are related with different behaviours and consequences. The convention of working with the concept of S-C-P has been started by Bain (1968). Under S-C-P framework, the market structure is projected to be the main determinant of industrial performance. It is contended that profitability would be relatively higher in highly concentrated industries or less competitive industries than highly competitive industries. A good deal of work in industrial organisation has sought to explain the performance differentials in terms of seller concentration. Seller concentration refers to the extent to which sales are concentrated in the hands of a small number of firms. Market structure usually refers to a set of variables that are important determinants of behaviour and conduct of the constituent firms of the industry. All scholars in the field of industrial organisation agree that there exists a set of variables which determine the conduct of firms in the markets. The main features which indicate the market structure are—concentration and concentration ratios, product differentiation, barriers to entry of new firms, growth rate of market demand, price elasticity of market demand etc. The market structure is supposed to determine the behaviour of buyers and sellers. Market behaviour refers to the decisions of the firms regarding which product to produce, prices and outputs, distribution, advertising strategy and R&D activity etc. Industrial organisation generally predicts the conduct of firms or sellers between two extremes—pure monopoly and perfect competition. Moreover, the movement from one extreme towards the other is supposed to bring in changes in performance. In other words, performance is supposed to be a function of all the aspects of conduct as well as the elements of market structure. The diagrammatic representation of S-C-P framework is given in Table 4.3.

Table 4.3 : Diagrammatical Representation of S-C-P Framework

Structure	Conduct	Performance
Perfect competition	Marginal cost pricing	Efficiency and normal profits
Non-perfect competition	Marginal cost pricing	Inefficiency and above normal profits

Theoretically, in perfectly competitive markets, there are a large number of firms and the demand is infinitely elastic. There is a very low level of concentration and no entry barriers or product differentiation. In the long run, price equals marginal cost and also equals average cost and producers make normal profits. As the competitive firm has so many rivals, its action will not affect the price and production policies of its competitors. At the other extreme, under monopoly, there is single firm and high seller concentration and very high entry barriers. The price is above marginal cost which results in super normal profits. However, these two extremes are rarely practical. In the real world, firms may be located along the range between these two rather theoretical extremes. The profitability is expected to rise from normal to supernormal levels as the movement is made from industries with large number of firms to industries with small number of firms. Imperfect competition refers to a situation in which there is neither absolute monopoly nor perfect competition. An oligopolistic market consists of a few sellers while there are only two suppliers under duopoly. A practical form of imperfect competition is monopolistic competition which is a blend of monopoly and competition. This type of market structure has a relatively large number of sellers of similar products (but not identical) and poses some degree of control over their selling prices. Instead of emphasis on price differences, the main focus under this type of competition is on product differentiation and advertising. To sum up, according to structure-conduct-performance paradigm, the departure from the competitive market structure will lead to higher rate of return. The anticipated relationship between market structure variables and financial performance is shown in Table 4.4.

Table 4.4 : Characteristics of Market Structure and its Relationship with Profitability

Market structure/ Market characteristics	Perfect competition	Monopolistic competition	Oligopoly	Duopoly	Monopoly	Relationship with profit
Seller concentration	Low	Low	High	High	Highest	Positive
Product differentiation	Absent	High	High or Low	High or Low	High or Low	Positive
Height of entry barriers	Absent	Low	High	High	High	Positive
Profitability	Normal	Above Normal	Above Normal	Above Normal	Super Normal	—

Source: Modified from Jones and Cockerill (1985).

Apart from the relationships between structural variables and performance, Table 4.3 also shows the impact of different market forms on profitability. Thus, for example, duopoly form of market is characterised by a high degree of seller concentration, a high degree of product differentiation and higher entry barriers, which is expected to lead to above normal profits. In brief, the relationship between market structure and profitability is postulated along the following lines:

— Profitability tends to be higher in those markets where (other thing being equal) seller concentration is higher;
— Profitability tends to be higher in those markets where (other things being equal) entry barriers are high;
— Profitability tends to be higher in those markets where (other things being equal) product differentiation is high.

Elements of Market Structure

As has been mentioned earlier, market structure refers to a set of variables which significantly affect the member firms of an industry. The majority of market structure-performance studies have sought to explain the causes of differential performance in terms of structural and other market characteristics. However, the variables employed in the structure-performance model vary considerably and differences also exist in respect of definition and measurement of variables between individual studies. Basically, there are two important elements of market structure which are emphasised in the S-C-P paradigm, viz. concentration and barriers to entry. By and large, the increasing level of seller concentration and high entry barriers are related to high profitability.

Bain (1951) identified seller concentration to be the main element of market structure. He found that high seller concentration was highly related to supra-normal profits. Later, Bain (1956) argued that high concentration as well as high entry barriers contribute to produce high profits. Bain (1968) considered four elements of market structure—seller concentration, buyer concentration, product differentiation and entry conditions. Seller concentration was held to facilitate non-competitive behaviour while buyer concentration was considered to work against such behaviour. Product differentiation was held to change the focus of firms from price to non-price competition and it was supposed to result in diversified actions of sellers different from each other.

Concerning entry conditions, it was argued that if the new competitors could enter an industry easily, the established firms would not be able to maintain prices above costs and earn supranormal profits. Many researchers have identified the marker share as an important element of market structure and other elements have shown to occupy secondary place (Shepherd, 1972; 1979).

Concentration and its Measurement

Industrial concentration is an important element of market structure. It refers to the extent to which the market for a particular product is in the hands of the few largest member firms of the industry. It indicates the state of competitive conditions prevailing in an industry. The competitive conditions may range from perfect competition to pure monopoly *via* oligopoly and duopoly. Various degrees of imperfect competition are represented between the two extremes. Moreover, the number of sellers may vary greatly between these two extremes of competition range. The smaller the number of sellers in a market, the larger, on average, will be the fractions of market share held by individual sellers. Besides any given percentage gain in sales by one seller at the expense of others results in more noticeable loss to each of the others and is more likely to invite retaliation.

Concentration Measures

Various measures of concentration have been used in the literature. On theoretical considerations, the use of Herfindahl Index has been indicated as the most promising measure of concentration. The Herfindahl Index, derived by O.C. Herfindahl for the U.S. Steel industry, is the sum of the squares of the sizes of firms in a market, in which sizes are expressed as a proportion of total market sales, or assets or employment. In mathematical notation:

$$\text{Herfindahl Index} = \Sigma (X_i / T)^2 \quad (i = 1,2,3, \ldots n)$$

where T represents total market sales, X_i represents the sales of individual firm i, and n is the number of firms in the market. Under pure competition, the index would equal zero. Under monopoly it would be equal to one.

Though Herfindahl Index is a better measure in the sense that it uses all the available information in the market, it is difficult to compute because of lack of data. In India the information on market shares of all the companies is not available to calculate this index. Centre for Monitoring Indian Economy (CMIE)'s publication *Market and Market Shares* provides information on the market shares of companies across a large number of product lines but all the companies are not covered by it due to the non-availability of data. Moreover, its market classification is not consistent over the years. This makes the use of Herfindahl Index impossible. Hence, we incorporated 4-firms concentration ratio for the purpose of this study. To work out the four-firm concentration ratio, the information on the shares of the four largest firms have been drawn from the CMIE's publication *Market and Market Shares*. This publication provides information on market shares of a large number of companies/units as a percentage of the total sales of the concerned industry. This information is arranged systematically beginning from the largest to the lowest. We simply added the percentage market shares of the largest four firms to construct four-firms concentration ratios.

Concentration Profitability

As discussed earlier, by and large, a significant and positive relationship is reported between concentration and profit. Weiss (1974) reviewed as many as 46 studies of the relationship between concentration and profitability in the United States, Britain, Canada and Japan and reported that majority of these studies revealed a significant and positive relationship. This finding has also been supported by studies in India and other developing countries. Table 4.5 enlists the studies of the relationship between profitability and concentration conducted in developing countries countries. It also shows profit measures used and their respective findings in brief. The finding of concentration-profitability

Table 4.5 : Studies of the Relationship Between Profitability and Concentration in Developing Countries

Country	Study	Profit Measure	Concentration-Profitability Relationship
India	Gupta (1968)	One year's Profit	Positive but not Statistically Significant
	Walgreen (1971)	rate as above	Positive but not Statistically Significant
	Sawhney and Sawhney (1973)	Gross and Net PCM 5 years' average	Positive and Significant at 5 per cent level
	Katrak (1980)	Gross PCM	Positive and significant at 5 per cent level
	Siddharthan and Dasgupta (1983)	PAT as per cent of Net worth 3 Years' average, 1975-78	Positive but not Statistically Significant
	Aggarwal (1992)	PCM and ROCE average for 3 periods 1974-78, 1982-86, 1973-86	Positive and statistically significant for PCM but not statistically significant for ROCE
Pakistan	White (1974)	PBT/Networth (2 years)	Positive and significant at 5 per cent level
	Sharwany (1976)	Rate of Return on Capital (4 years)	Positive and significant at 5 per cent level
	Amjad (1977)	Net PCM single year and 3 years average (1965-67)	Positive and significant at 5 per cent level
Malaysia	Gan & Tham (1977)	Gross PCM, 4 years average (1968-71)	Positive and significant at 10 per cent level
	Gan (1978)	As above	Positive and significant at 10 per cent level
Brazil	Connor & Muller (1982)	Profit as per cent of equity (1972)	Positive and significant at 5 per cent level
	Newfarmer and Mueller (1975)	Broad earnings' (including technology fees) of US manufacturing affiliates as percentage of their equity (1972)	Positive
Mexico	Newfarmer and Muller (1975)	As above (1972)	Positive
	Connor and Muller (1982)	Profit as per cent of equity (1972)	Positive and significant at 5 per cent level

(Contd.)

Table 4.5 *(Contd.)*

Country	Study	Profit Measure	Concentration-Profitability Relationship
Korea	Nam (1975)	NP-Gross Capital Ratio and NP-net sales ratio single years and 3 years average 1967-69	Positive
	Jeong and Masson (1990)	ROA (1976-81)	Positive and significant at 5 per cent level
Kenya	House (1973)	Gross and Net PCM (1963)	Positive and significant at 5 per cent level
	House (1976)	Gross and Net PCM (1967)	Positive and significant at 5 per cent level
Philippines	Lindsey (1977)	Gross PCM (1970)	Positive and significant at 5 per cent level
South Africa	Reekie (1984)	Net Oupput less wages as a per cent of Gross Output	Positive

Source : Modified and Updated from Kirkpatrick *et al.* (1985).

relationship has had two implications, discussed in succeeding pragraphs.

Concentration-Collusion-Profitability

The main interpretation drawn from the positive and significant concentration-profit relationship is that concentration will facilitate collusion, whether tacit or explicit and by virtue of collusive and monopolistic practices, the level of profitability will rise with concentration. This hypothesis is derived from oligopoly theory which is based on the effectiveness of collusion. Bain (1951) was the first to argue that successful collusion between firms would result in joint profit maximisation. In highly concentrated firms, there are fewer firms having hold on the total market share and these fewer firms may indulge in collusive and monopolistic practices and earn monopoly profits. The ability to collude would increase with concentration and so other things being equal monopoly profit rates could be expected to increase with concentration as collusion become progressivelv more successful.

However, there is another school of thought which provides a different explanation for this relationship (discussed below).

Concentration-Efficiency-Profitability

According to this view, the positive and significant association between concentration and profitability is not due to collusive and monopolistic practices rather the finding of positive and significant relationship between concentration and profitability is supposed to be due to the superior efficiency of large firms, economies of scale, superior management, superior products or good luck.

However, certain careful studies on market share (e.g. Ravenscraft, 1983) revealed that concentration-profitability relationship appeared to be mainly a matter of market share. Regarding the relationship between concentration and profitability, Weiss (1991) observed that to have a better basis for judging the effects of concentration, its relationship should be linked to price rather than to profits. In order to clarify the phenomenon, he initiated research on concentration and price. The results revealed that concentration usually raised price. By establishing the link between market concentration and price, he and his associates verified the existence of a relationship between industry structure and performance which had eluded the researchers in the concentration-profitability studies. He further argued that exceptions to this finding were attributable to factors such as unanticipated inflation and/or price controls etc.

Market Share

A number of research scholars have stated the market share to be the leading element of market structure and it has been widely employed in regression models along with the main structural variables. It shows the extent of a firm's control over the market and indicates its position in the market. Many studies have produced findings showing a positive correlation between market share and profit rates. The other elements (concentration and entry barriers) have been shown to play relatively much weaker roles (Shepherd, 1972,1979). Market share's role derives from the fundamental theory of monopoly. A pure monopoly (market share of 100 per cent) controls the entire market. The monopolist's demand is as inelastic as that of the entire market, and so its ability to raise price and influence other market outcomes reflect a full exploitation of that inelasticity.

Concentration vs. Market Share

As regarding the importance of concentration as an element of market structure, concentration is given secondary importance to market share. To take an example, in an industry with 90 per cent 4-firm concentration ratio, a particular company might be having a market share of 50 per cent of the total business in the industry, and other three getting the rest of 40 per cent. In such a case, the so-called particular company is likely to show better performance on account of its own 50 per cent share rather than due to the fact that it belongs to a market with very high 4-firm concentration ratio.

Barriers to Entry

This is another important element of market structure. As mentioned earlier, it was Bain (1956) who first argued that besides high concentration, high barriers to entry contributed to produce high profits. He identified scale economies, capital requirements, and product differentiation as the possible sources of entry barriers. However, the fourth one absolute cost advantages of established firms was found least important in his sample. The extent of competition in an industry or market is expected to be influenced by the number of new entrants. The barriers to entry might make markets imperfect, which might tend to raise the profitability of the existing firms. The variables of the entry barriers have been discussed in the next section.

Control Variables

Many studies revealed that market structure variables explained only a small portion of profitability variations between markets.

This suggested the need to include other variables in the model that might contribute to explain the profit differences. Apart from structural variables, a number of control variables have been employed in the model in the more recent studies. Other variables that are included in certain studies are—import ratio, export ratio, advertising-sales ratio, R&D-sales ratio, capital intensity variables, risk, economies of scale, capacity utilisation etc. Capital intensity and economies of scale are also used as the indicators of entry barriers. Inter-industry studies that failed to allow for the influences of such variables have been criticised on the grounds that these reflect biased results. In this study, a number of control variables have been used in the regression models in order to disintegrate their impact on performance. They will be discussed in the subsequent chapters of their use.

Contribution of Bain and Weiss

Bain is described as the main contributor to shape the field of industrial organisation in its present form. He observed that technical factors determine structure and the structure then influences behaviour and performance. He analysed the profitability very closely and tried to explain the concentration-profitability relationship. Firstly, he regarded the concentration as the key determinant of market power and profitability. Later he found the barriers to be the decisive determinant of profitability. He suggested that barriers and degree of concentration were highly correlated.

Although Joe Bain is acknowledged as the originator of the structure-conduct-performance format, Leonard W. Weiss is counted among those responsible scholars who undertook painstaking research on the subject and developed a systematic body of knowledge on this agenda. In order to clarify the phenomenon, he initiated research on concentration and price. The results revealed that concentration usually raised price. By establishing the link between market concentration and price, he and his associates verified the existence of a relationship between industry structure and performance which had eluded the researchers in the concentration-profitability studies. The link between S-C-P also served as the basis of public policy.

Basic Models for Testing Structure-Performance Relationship

Various models have been developed to test how market structure may affect profitability. There are several variations of them. The most common and familiar are shown here.

1. Profit rate = f (MS, C, Size, Adv. Int., Growth)

Where profit rate is ROE or ROA, MS is market share, C is 4-firms concentration in the market, size is a measure of the firm's absolute size, Adv. Int. represents the firm's advertising expenditure as a percentage of its sales, and Growth is a variable for the firm's growth rate.

2. Profit rate = f (MS, C, HEB, MEB, Growth)

Where HEB and MEB are dummy variables for high and medium entry barriers.

These equations are fitted to cross-section data for 100 or more large industrial firms, across a range of industries. In order to reflect basic conditions rather than yearly fluctuations, data are pooled up for various periods. Several other structural variables are occasionally included in the model. These include vertical structure, diversification, leverage, producer-consumer goods differences, foreign control etc. The relationships can be assumed to be linear with simple coefficient or curvilinear relationships can be tested by converting some or all variables to logarithms (Shepherd, 1979).

Summary

This chapter has outlined the main relationships in the structure-conduct-performance model. The elements of market structure and their expected relationship with profitability have been described. The S-C-P paradigm seeks to explain and predict the performance of an industry as a consequence of its structure. The different forms of market are—perfect competition, monopolistic competition, oligopoly, duopoly and monopoly. The important elements of market structure are—seller concentration, product differentiation, entry barriers, market share, size etc. Apart from these, various control variables are also included in model to test the structure-performance relationship. Various control variables are—risk, leverage, foreign control, diversification etc. The contribution of Bain and Weiss in the field of industrial organisation economics has also been summarised. Finally, the commonly used models to test structure-performance relationship are provided.

5

INDUSTRY CATEGORY AND PERFORMANCE

Introduction

This chapter analyses the performance of companies in terms of industry categories. Hypotheses regarding inter-industry performance differences are developed and tested. The analysis has been carried out for three different classifications of industries as defined in Chapter 3. In all, data of 187 companies have been analysed. The use-based classification of industries consists of 159 companies grouped into four industry categories. The Input-based classification of industries comprises of 115 companies divided into three industry groups. And the Commodity/Activity-based classification of industries contains 182 companies spread over 21 industry groups. The samples of Use-based and Input-based classification of industries were made up with companies in Commodity/Activity-based classification of industries, however, 5 more companies were added in the categories which were underrepresented (see Table 3.1, Chapter 3).

While forming sample for Commodity/Activity-based classification of industries, it was envisaged to include 10 companies in each industry, but it could not be possible due to sampling technique (detailed in Chapter 3). Although number of companies in tobacco industry is 4, it covers 89.4 per cent of total industry sales in 1991 and 89.9 per cent in 1981. Six companies in paint industry embrace 76.7 per cent of industry sales in 1991 and sample companies in aluminium industry show 49.3 per cent and 83 per cent of total industry sales in 1991 and 1981 respectively. Similarly, samples of jute and vanaspati industries cover 20.8 per cent and 18 per cent of 1991's industry sales respectively (CMIE, March 1992, June 1983). Electricity companies in this study cover virtually 100 per cent of private sector sales of the industry over the period under study.* Fertiliser industry is operating mainly in public sector.

This study measures the company performance by incorporating profitability and growth dimensions (The choice of performance measures has been discussed in detail in Chapter 3). The five indicators of performance selected for the study are Return on Equity (ROE), Return on Assets (ROA), Growth in Sales (GSALES), Growth in Total Net Assets (GTNA) and Growth in Dividend (GDIV) (computation formulae of these variables are provided in Chapter 3). ROE and ROA have been employed as profitability indicators while GSALES, GTNA and GDIV have been taken to represent growth performance of companies. One Way Analysis of performance has been applied, firstly, on five performance indicators separately for three different classification systems of industries. Later on, a composite index of performance has been constructed to do the same analysis in a precise form.

Hypotheses on Industry Category and Performance

The industry characteristics have vital concern in the analysis of performance of firms. Companies operating in new and expanding industries are likely to perform better than those operating in traditional and declining industries. Many studies have revealed that some factors allow firms in some industries to be in a better position to implement their strategies successfully and profitably. Consequently, these firms may be reflecting better performance on account of certain favourable industrial characteristics which affect all the firms in a particular industry. In India, as also in many other countries, different industries are subjected to varied policies of the Government. The nature and rates of taxation paid

* Electricity is a concurrent subject in the Constitution of India. Its development is a joint responsibility of the Central and State Governments. Nearly two-third of the power generating capacity in the country is in the hands of State Governments. As on 31 March, 1994, the State Sector owned 50528 mw of capacity, the Central sector 23234 mw and the private sector only 2950 mw (Industrial Survey, SEOD, August 1995).

by companies are determined by government policies and sometimes Government favours an industry by providing incentives in terms of reduced taxes, financial support, subsidies, and other such facilities. The development of industries is also influenced by government regulations. The sale of particular class of goods may be limited (e.g. alcoholic drink, petrol), similarly, prices may be controlled, thus influencing profitability and growth of companies. Further, trade policies towards imports and exports in India are not same for all the industries.

Sometimes governments intervene the free operation of market forces to maintain the composition of industrial activities that is best suited to the needs of the country. For example, the erstwhile Monopolies and Restrictive Trade Practices Act, 1969 was a piece of economic legislation which sought to ensure that the operation of the economic system did not result in the concentration of economic power to the common detriment. Similarly, the benefits of industrial licensing may go to few industries resulting in their disproportionate growth. Such things may contribute to varied performance of companies operating in different industries.

Many researchers have provided empirical support to the phenomenon of inter-industry performance differences. Porter (1985) reports that all industries do not offer equal opportunities for sustained profitability. Porter (1980) asserts that the overall firm performance is influenced by the characteristics of the various industries to which a firm belongs. Many researchers have stated that industry effects explained a significant portion of the variation in the company profitability (Schmalensee, 1985; Kessides, 1990; Amato and Wilder, 1990). The industry-wise analysis of performance of the companies, as is conducted by Reserve Bank of India, reveals the existence of varied growth rates in different industries (*R.B.I. Bulletins*, March 1992, November 1991 and various other issues). Hence, inter-industry research can help a great deal in formulating sound theory and making policies for specific industries.

Statistical Results : Analysis for the Five Performance Measures Separately

This section presents empirical results of the analyses of inter-industry performance variations for three different classification systems adopted in the study. The findings are based on 11-year observations of five performance indicators. The empirical analysis in this chapter involves three stages. At first stage, ANOVA has been used to study the performance dispersion among different categories within each classification of industries and to test the level of significance for such dispersion. At the second stage, the information on five variables has been condensed with the help of Factor Analysis and a composite index of performance is constructed. The analysis conducted at the first stage is repeated on condensed information. Pairwise comparisons have been done at both the stages by using Tukey's Test of multiple comparisons.

Input-Based Classification : One Way Analysis of Variance and Pairwise Comparison

This section contains the results of preliminary analysis of industry category and performance by Input-based classification systems of industries over the period 1980-81 to 1990-91. The sample for this classification contains 115 companies spread over three industry segments. Table 5.1 shows the results of ANOVA for the five performance indicators separately. Number of observations, however, have to be truncated on ROE variable in some industries due to computation problems on account of negative denominator*. The F-ratios depicted in the Table provide a test of the strength of significance of inter-industry differentials within the industry classification.

---

* ROE is computed by *dividing* 'profit after interest, taxes and preference dividend' *by* 'Net worth'. But sometimes, Net Worth is nil or negative due to accumulation of losses, and in such instances it sounds nonsense to compute return on nil net worth or on accumulated losses.

Table 5.1 : One-way Analysis of Variance on Industry and Performance : Input-Based Industry Classification

Performance	Agro	Metal	Chemical	Overall	F-Ratio
ROE Mean	11.05	13.24	9.61	11.04	
SD	17.61	9.87	20.82	17.40	0.30
NO	51	23	36	110	
ROA Mean	11.20	12.06	11.23	11.38	
SD	7.65	5.14	3.59	6.11	0.18
NO	56	23	36	115	
GSALES Mean	11.52	19.89	14.31	14.07	
SD	6.15	24.68	6.54	12.61	3.78^b
NO	56	23	36	115	
GTNA Mean	13.31	19.09	15.95	15.29	
SD	5.91	12.73	7.97	8.52	4.12^b
NO	56	23	36	115	
GDIV Mean	38.45	17.53	13.81	26.55	
SD	74.63	84.51	47.76	70.02	1.61
NO	56	23	36	115	

Note: Significance levels: a = 1%; b = 5%; c = 10%

Table 5.1 provides the results of the analysis of industry category and performance for Input-based classification. Of the three industry categories, the Metal-based industry scores the highest on all the performance variables save GDIV, on which its mean value is below even the grand mean. It may be dividend policy by virtue of which companies in this industry are performing well on all the indicators of performance except GDIV.* The Agro-based industry has the highest level on GDIV indicator and stands next to the highest levels on ROE. However, its performance is the lowest on ROA, GSALES and GTNA variables. The Chemical-based industry group is the poorest on

* Dividend policy decides as to how much profits are to be distributed to the shareholders and how much are to be retained by the company for the ploughing back. Such decisions are supposed to have a direct impact on the growth of a company.

ROE and GDIV indicators. Equally, its mean values are below the corresponding overall mean values. However, it stands next to the highest level on ROA, GSALES and GTNA variables. The F-ratios indicate that the null hypothesis of inter-industry performance differences is rejected on only GSALES and GTNA at 5 per cent level of significance. The industries within this classification do not differ significantly from one another on ROE, ROA and GDIV measures of performance.

Pairwise Comparison

Although the one way ANOVA has rejected the null hypothesis of equal means of all industry categories for GSALES and GTNA variables, but we do not know where exactly the differences lie between groups. To know this, Tukey's test of multiple comparisons has been employed to compare the performance of three industry groups with one another. The outcome of Tukey's test is given in Table 5.2.

Table 5.2 : Tukey's Test of Multiple Comparison of Industry Performances : Input-Based Industry Classification

(elements are differences between means)

Performance Variable	Pairs of Industry Groups* Being Compared			HSD (at 5% level)
	A - M	A - C	M - C	
ROE	– 2.19	1.45	3.64	10.27
ROA	– 0.86	– 0.03	0.84	3.37
GSALES	– 8.37**	– 2.79	5.58	7.59
GTNA	– 5.78**	– 2.64	3.14	4.82
GDIV	20.92	24.64	3.72	40.45

Note: * A, M, & C stand respectively for Agro, Metal and Chemical based industry groups.

** Significant at 5% level of significance.

Evidently there is significant difference only between group A and group M in respect of only GSALES and GTNA. To be more specific, the sales and net assets growth rates of Agro-based group are significantly less than that of Metal-based group of companies. No other pair shows statistically significant difference.

Use-Based Classification : One-way Analysis of Variance and Pairwise Comparison

Table 5.3 shows the results of ANOVA on industry category and performance for Use-based classification. Of the four industry categories, the capital goods industry has the highest levels of ROE, ROA, GSALES and GTNA measures of performance. Although this industry does not have the highest level on GDIV variable, it stands next to the highest. As cited above, may be the companies in this industry are performing well on account of its dividend policies which have direct bearing on the growth of a company. In other words, its dividend decisions may be contributing to its being best on all the other variables considered here. One reason of the highest performance of this industry may be due to its getting special attention in Sixth Plan (1980-85). The Basic goods industry has poor levels of profitability variables, i.e. ROE and ROA and its mean performance on these two variables is even below the overall mean performance. However, the mean performance on growth variables of this category is higher than the overall mean performance. The Intermediate goods industry performs at the lowest levels as regarding profitability measures. On growth variables also, its performance is very poor except on GDIV variable where it has comparatively the highest level. The performance picture of consumer goods industry is inverse to that of the first category of Use-based classification of industry. This group stands next to the highest level on profitability measures but the same scores consistently the lowest on growth variables. The F-ratios indicate that the null hypothesis of inter-industry performance differences is rejected on only ROA at 1 per cent level of significance.

Table 5.3 : One-way Analysis of Variance on Industry and Performance : Use Based Industry Classification

Performance	Basic	Inter-mediate	Capital	Consumer	Overall	F-Ratio
ROE Mean	6.94	4.20	15.05	13.35	9.52	
SD	39.70	24.42	8.90	9.64	24.52	1.527
NO	38	40	16	58	152	
ROA Mean	9.22	8.96	12.83	12.23	10.67	
SD	3.66	5.08	5.30	6.56	5.63	4.843[a]
NO	40	42	16	61	159	
GSALES	15.08	13.27	19.92	12.71	14.18	
Mean						
SD	10.98	6.39	29.17	7.26	12.07	1.681
NO	40	42	16	61	159	
GTNA Mean	15.62	14.80	18.14	14.27	15.14	
SD	6.35	7.38	15.01	6.99	8.08	1.043
NO	40	42	16	61	159	
GDIV Mean	27.41	30.20	27.43	16.85	24.10	
SD	73.83	83.57	97.56	47.75	70.44	0.357
NO	40	42	16	61	159	

Note: Significance levels: a = 1%; b = 5%; c = 10%

Pairwise Comparison

Pairwise comparison of industry categories is done by applying Tukey's test of multiple comparison. It shows that only Capital goods segment is significantly different from Basic goods and Intermediate goods in respect of only ROA variable of profitability. In other words, the ROA performance of only Capital goods segment is significantly higher than that of Basic and Intermediate segments of Use-based classification of industries. No other pair shows statistically significant difference (see Table 5.4).

Table 5.4 : Tukey's Test of Multiple Comparison of Industry Performance : Use-Based Classification

(Elements are Differences between Means)

Performance Variable	Pairs of Industry Groups* Being Compared						
	A - B	A - C	A - D	B - C	B - D	C - D	HSD (at 5% level)
ROE	2.74	– 8.11	– 6.11	– 10.85	– 9.15	1.70	16.03
ROA	0.26	– 3.61*	– 3.01	– 3.87**	– 3.27	0.60	3.53
GSALES	1.81	– 4.84	2.37	– 6.65	0.56	7.21	7.78
GTNA	0.81	– 2.52	1.35	– 3.34	0.54	3.87	5.24
GDIV	– 2.79	– 0.01	10.56	2.77	13.35	10.58	45.97

Note: * A, B, C and D stand respectively for Basic, Intermediate, Capital and Consumer Industries.

** Significant at 5% level of significance.

Commodity/Activity-Based Classification : One-way Analysis of Variance and Pairwise Comparison

The perusal of Table 5.5 reveals that none of the 21 industries is consistently ranking best on all the five measures of performance. However, paint and sugar industries show consistently higher than the overall mean performance on all the five measures. Inversely, jute and paper industries are below the overall mean values on all the pointers of performance. Although automobile, iron and steel, pharmaceutical, tea and tyre and tube industries are not showing above average performance on all the variables, these can be placed next to the good performing industries as their performance on four of the five measures is good. Similarly, aluminium, cotton textile and construction industries are poor on all the variables except one and these can be categorised as next to the poorly performing industries. The rest of the industries are showing mixed results on different performance indicators.

Table 5.5 : One-way Analysis of Variance on Industry and Performance : Commodity/Activity-Based Industry Classification

Industry	ROE	ROA	GSALES	GTNA	GDIV
Aluminium					
Mean	7.25	7.34	20.59	11.08	8.50
Sd	13.24	5.6	20.62	4.84	10.05
No.	4	6	6	6	6
Automobile					
Mean	10.57	10.71	17.84	18.02	0.22
Sd	9.78	3.91	9.00	6.65	33.17
No.	10	10	10	10	10
Cement					
Mean	– 13.34	8.22	17.06	17.15	– 6.29
Sd	74.21	3.54	9.93	7.34	49.76
No.	10	10	10	10	10
Cotton Textile					
Mean	10.61	8.47	10.10	10.88	9.13
Sd	7.44	4.84	8.10	5.15	25.06
No.	8	10	10	10	10
Electrical Machinery					
Mean	12.10	13.16	11.92	15.92	– 2.25
Sd	8.14	5.89	6.78	5.38	26.27
No.	9	9	9	9	9
Fertilisers					
Mean	19.73	11.11	11.64	11.35	55.51
Sd	15.85	3.24	5.65	4.36	70.63
No.	6	6	6	6	6
Iron & Steel					
Mean	12.56	10.36	12.35	16.92	31.91
Sd	8.14	3.37	10.76	5.99	43.04
No.	10	10	10	10	10
Jute					
Mean	– 15.75	2.03	8.05	9.99	5.56
Sd	33.16	4.76	5.82	4.85	38.22
No.	7	8	8	8	8
Man Made Fibre					
Mean	2.74	10.37	15.59	17.93	-4.22
Sd	29.99	3.41	6.73	9.20	32.60
No.	14	14	14	14	14

(contd.)

Table 5.5 *(contd.)*

Paints					
Mean	13.26	11.59	13.58	16.40	30.74
Sd	6.38	3.73	2.46	3.49	56.96
No.	6	6	6	6	6
Paper					
Mean	8.75	8.54	10.35	9.21	1.44
Sd	9.60	3.25	5.00	5.61	64.12
No.	10	10	10	10	10
Pharmaceuticals					
Mean	10.96	12.27	14.56	15.66	3.88
Sd	8.50	4.15	8.50	9.33	28.20
No.	10	10	10	10	10
Sugar					
Mean	16.83	11.63	12.99	15.76	46.52
Sd	5.75	2.72	4.72	3.23	62.83
No.	9	10	10	10	10
Tea					
Mean	20.70	22.03	10.31	17.15	38.48
Sd	10.44	8.30	4.94	6.50	47.86
No.	10	10	10	10	10
Tobacco					
Mean	17.55	11.11	13.38	8.76	17.26
Sd	8.73	3.17	4.90	4.29	7.59
No.	4	4	4	4	4
Tyre & Tube					
Mean	12.93	10.54	13.62	13.37	103.87
Sd	7.54	3.90	6.28	5.55	135.84
No.	9	10	10	10	10
Vanaspati					
Mean	11.02	9.98	14.27	14.70	14.95
Sd	6.47	4.46	7.42	9.47	33.51
No.	4	4	4	4	4
Construction					
Mean	11.85	8.43	4.59	10.05	-18.20
Sd	8.82	5.31	9.42	4.96	28.35
No.	8	9	9	9	9
Electricity					
Mean	15.60	9.29	15.76	16.92	10.25
Sd	7.93	2.20	2.07	2.29	4.23
No.	7	7	7	7	7

(contd.)

Table 5.5 *(contd.)*

Shipping					
Mean	13.51	5.04	12.56	9.97	71.17
Sd	5.99	7.03	15.06	12.45	91.24
No.	6	9	9	9	9
Trading					
Mean	15.07	10.24	9.91	12.05	46.31
Sd	4.94	3.07	8.74	6.00	23.31
No.	10	10	10	10	10
Overall					
Mean	9.76	10.22	12.81	14.07	21.79
Sd	23.15	5.68	2.79	7.05	62.13
No.	171	182	182	182	182
F-Ratios	1.37	6.09a	1.43	2.07a	2.54a

Note: Significant levels: a = 1%; b = 5%; c = 10%

Table 5.6 below summarises the findings of this sub-section.

Table 5.6 : Brief View of Industry Performance : Commodity/Activity-based Industry Classification

Performance	Industry
Good	Paint, Sugar
Next to the Good	Automobile, Iron and Steel, Pharmaceuticals, Tea, Tyre and Tube
Poor	Jute, Paper
Next to the Poor	Aluminium, Cotton Textile, Construction
Mixed	Cement, Electrical Machinery, Fertilisers, Man-made Fibre, Tobacco, Vanaspati, Electricity, Shipping, Trading

Good performance here means the performance above overall average on all the five indicators. Inversely, poor performance indicates below overall average performance on all the measures. 'Next to the Good' performance group consists of those industries which are good on all measures except one, and inversely 'Next to the Poor' infers to those which are poor on all performance indicators save one. The mixed performance here refers to a blend of good and poor performance on different variables.

For this classification of industries, the null hypothesis of performances is disapproved on only ROA, GTNA and GDIV indicators of performance at 1 per cent level of significance.

Pairwise Comparison

Tukey's test of multiple comparison on different indicators of performance reveals that no pair is statistically and significantly different on ROE and GTNA variables of performance. The findings of Tukey's test are summarised in Table 5.7 to give a brief view of results of pairwise comparison of performance of different industries within Commodity/Activity based classification of industries, on the five performance measures.

Table 5.7 : Summarised Findings of Tukey's Test of Multiple Comparison on Performance : Commodity/Activitiy-based Industry Classification

Performance Indicator	Significant Differences Between Means at 5 per cent Level of Significance
ROE	No pair is significantly different from one another.
ROA	Tea significantly higher than : Jute, Shipping, Aluminium, Cement, Construction, Cotton Textile, Paper, Electricity, Vanaspati, Trading, Iron and Steel, Man Made Fibre, Tyre and Tube, Automobile, Tobacco, Fertiliser, Paint, Sugar, Pharmaceutical, Electrical Machinery. Jute is significantly less than: Trading, Iron and Steel, Man-made Fibre, Tyre and Tube, Automobile, Tobacco, Fertiliser, Paint, Sugar, Pharmaceutical, Electrical Machinery, Tea.
GSALES	Aluminium significantly higher than construction.
GTNA	No pair is significantly different from one another.
GDIV	Tyre and Tube significantly higher than : Construction, Cement, Man-made Fibre, Electrical machinery, Automobile.

Construction of Composite Index of Performance

So far we have sought to analyse the performance differences in various industry groupings on each of the five indicators of performance separately. Our performance indicators cover two dimensions, viz. profitability and growth. ROE and ROA are the indicators of profitability while GSALES, GTNA and GDIV are the representatives of growth. As is evident from the foregoing analysis, there is no consistency in performance virtually on all the five variables. Almost all industries show inconsistent results across the five indicators of performance. It is, therefore, rather a formidable task to say with confidence as to which industry is performing the best. Apart from this, profitability and growth may be two divergent objectives. Berle and Means (1932) observed that ownership and management were separated to a great extent in large companies. Consequently there may be divergent (and sometimes conflicting too) objectives in such companies. As for example, profitability is assumed to be the only objective of business while Penrose (1959) considered growth to be the main objective of managerially controlled firms. In order to have a brief picture of results of our analysis and to resolve the problem of divergent objectives, a composite index of performance is constructed by using the technique of Factor Analysis (see Bourgeois, 1980, 1985; and Hamilton and Shergill, 1993 for a similar approach). The factor analysis is done for all the three industry classification systems separately. This technique extracted two performance factors in each case. The empirical results of factor analysis for developing composite performance index have been presented in Tables 5.8 to 5.22 followed by discussion thereof.

Factor Analysis for Input-Based Industry Classification

Table 5.8 : Pearson Product Moment Correlations Among Performance Variables for Input-based Industry Classification

Variable	ROE	ROA	GSALES	GTNA	GDIV
ROE	1.00				
ROA	0.52**	1.00			
GSALES	0.28*	0.09	1.00		
GTNA	0.28*	0.18	0.81**	1.00	
GDIV	0.33**	0.12	0.50**	0.37**	1.00

Note: * Significant at 0.01 Level.
** Significant at 0.001 Level.
No. of Cases 110

Table 5.9 : Factor Structure and Commonalities of Performance Variables for Input-based Industry Classification

Variables	Common-alities	Factor	Eigen value	% of variance	Cumulative
ROE	0.75117	1	2.44439	48.9	48.9
ROA	0.79531	2	1.25019	25.0	73.9
GSALES	0.88041				
GTNA	0.77771				
GDIV	0.48997				

Trace = 5.0

Table 5.10 : Varimax Rotated (Orthogonal) Factor Matrix of Performance Variables for Input-based Industry Classification

Variable	Factor I	Factor II
ROE	0.26972	0.82367
ROA	0.00825	0.89177
GSALES	0.93700	0.04950
GTNA	0.87469	0.11241
GDIV	0.67344	0.19092

Table 5.11 : Factor Score Coefficient Matrix of Performance Variables for Input-based Industry Classification

Variable	Factor	
	I-GRTH	II-PRTF
ROE	– 0.00090	0.54033
ROA	– 0.14260	0.63169
GSALES	0.45951	-0.11902
GTNA	0.41806	-0.06411
GDIV	0.30470	0.02473

Table 5.12 : Grand Means and Standard Deviations of Performance Variables for Input-based Industry Classification

Variable	Mean	Standard Deviation
ROE	11.04	17.40
ROA	11.72	5.96
GSALES	14.49	12.60
GTNA	15.60	8.52
GDIV	28.25	70.99

Note : No. of Cases = 110.

Factor Analysis for Use-based Industry Classification

Table 5.13 : Pearson Product Moment Correlations Among Performance Variables for Use-based Industry Classification

Variable	ROE	ROA	GSALES	GTNA	GDIV
ROE	1.00				
ROA	0.43**	1.00			
GSALES	0.22*	0.10	1.00		
GTNA	0.27**	0.19*	0.72**	1.00	
GDIV	0.27**	0.13	0.36**	0.40**	1.00

Note: * Significant at .01 1-tailed test.
** Significant at .001 1-tailed test.

Table 5.14 : Factor Structure and Commonalities of Performance Variables for Use-based Industry Classification

Variable	Commonalities	Factor	Eigen Value	% of Variance	Cumulative
ROE	0.69569	1	2.28334	45.7	45.7
ROA	0.74375	2	1.17862	23.6	69.2
GSALES	0.79216				
GTNA	0.79670				
GDIV	0.43366				

Table 5.15 : Varimax Rotated (Orthogonal) Factor Matrix of Performance Variables for Use-based Industry Classification

Variable	Factor I	Factor II
ROE	0.22845	0.80219
ROA	0.03190	0.86182
GSALES	0.88981	0.01985
GTNA	0.88275	0.13208
GDIV	0.62588	0.20479

Table 5.16 : Factor Score Coefficient Matrix of Performance Variables for Use-based Industry Classification

Variable	Factor	
	I-GRTH	II-PRTF
ROE	– 0.01830	0.56075
ROA	– 0.13439	0.63997
GSALES	0.47462	– 0.14158
GTNA	0.45109	– 0.05627
GDIV	0.30028	0.04336

Table 5.17 : Grand Means and Standard Deviations of Performance Variables for Use-based Industry Classification

Variable	Mean	Standard Deviation
ROE	9.52	24.52
ROA	11.00	5.47
GSALES	14.09	11.55
GTNA	15.45	8.08
GDIV	25.56	71.60

Note : No. of cases =152.

Factor Analysis for Commodity/Activity-based Industry Classification

Table 5.18 : Pearson Product Moment Correlations Among Performance Variables for Commodity/Activity-based Industry Classification

Variable	ROE	ROA	GSALES	GTNA	GDIV
ROE	1.00				
ROA	0.426a	1.00			
GSALES	0.201a	0.105	1.00		
GTNA	0.254a	0.201a	0.723a	1.00	
GDIV	0.259a	0.119	0.349a	0.380a	1.00

Note: [a] Significant at 1% Level.
[b] Significant at 5% Level.

Table 5.19 : Factor Structure and Commonalities of Performance Variables for Commodity/Activity-based Industry Classification

Variable	Commonalities	Factor	Eigen Value	% of Variance	Cumulative
ROE	0. 69658	1	2.25670	45.1	45.1
ROA	0.73409	2	1.18247	23.6	68.8
GSALES	0.79607				
GTNA	0.79363				
GDIV	0.41878				

Trace = 5.0

Table 5.20 : Varimax Rotated (Orthogonal) Factor Matrix of Performance Variables for Commodiy/Activity-based Industry Classification

Variable	Factor I	Factor II
ROE	0.21033	0.80768
ROA	0.04142	0.85579
GSALES	0.89205	0.01770
GTNA	0.88063	0.13462
GDIV	0.61771	0.19292

Table 5.21 : Factor Score Coefficient Matrix of Performance Variables for Commodity/Activity-based Industry Classification

Variable	Factor	
	I-GRTH	II-PRTF
ROE	– 0.02535	0.56882
ROA	– 0.12479	0.63390
GSALES	0.47846	– 0.14013
GTNA	0.45220	– 0.05059
GDIV	0.30025	0.03829

Table 5.22 : Grand Means and Standard Deviations of Performance Variables for Commodity/Activity-based Industry Classification

Variable	Mean	Standard Deviation
ROE	10.0766	22.9428
ROA	0.8151	5.2589
GSALES	13.6008	11.4715
GTNA	5.0562	7.9466
GDIV	28.1593	73.0236

Note : No. of Cases = 171.

As is evident from Tables 5.10, 5.15 and 5.20 above, the first factor for each of the three industry classifications is based on measures of growth (and is henceforth GRTH) and the second factor in all the three cases is based around profitability (PRTF). These factors were derived by using the SPSS/PC$^+$ package on computer. The criterion for accepting this two-factor solution in each case is that it explains 73.9 per cent, 69.2 per cent and 68.8 per cent of the total variance among all five performance measures respectively for Input, Use and Commodity/Activity-based classification of industries (Bourgeois, 1985; Zaltman and Burger, 1975).

For each company a vector of factor scores for GRTH and PRTF was calculated as follows:

$$GRTH = F.Z$$
$$PRTF = F.Z$$

where *F* is the factor score coefficient matrix (Tables 5.11, 5.16, 5.21) and *Z* is the vector of standardised values of the five variables which have been factor analysed (Rummel, 1970). For example, in case of Commodity/Activity-based industry classification, from the factor score coefficient matrix in Table 5.21, we constructed GRTH and PRTF of company "1" as follows:

$$GRTH1 = (-0.02535).Z_1+(-0.12479).Z_2+(0.47846).Z_3+ (0.45220).Z_4+(0.30025).Z_5$$

$$PRTF1 = (0.56882).Z_1+(0.63390).Z_2+(-0.14013).Z_3+(-0.05059).Z_4+(0.03829).Z_5$$

where Z_n represents the standardised values of variables ROE, ROA, GSALES, GTNA, and GDIV respectively. Thus Z_1 = (ROE of Company "1" *minus* the average ROE of all Companies) *divided by* the standard deviations of the average ROE for all companies. Similarly for Z_2 to Z_5. By applying this methodology, we calculated GRTH and PRTF as performance variables from all the five variables for each of the three-industry classification samples. In the subsequent analysis of performance, this methodology is applied throughout the rest of Chapters 5, 6 and 7 and discussion concentrates around these two composite variables.

Statistical Results : Analysis Using Composite Index of Performance

The analysis at the former stage does not provide a lucid picture of the performance and a fair comparison between industries' performances is rather a formidable task. For instance, in case of Commodity/Activity-based industry classification, automobile industry is ranking 1st on GTNA, 2nd on GSALES, 8th on ROA, 10th on ROE and 17th on GDIV variable. Here it is fairly difficult to say categorically as to whether it is the best, a good or a poorly performing industry. In order to resolve this problem, we have carried out the same analysis by using a composite index of performance. The performance is now described in terms of two factors, viz. GRTH and PRTF extracted through factor analysis. Now one can easily know whether an industry is best on both or one dimension of performance or is it a good, poor, or very poorly performing industry. The status of each industry regarding profitability and growth can easily be stated and a comparison can be made with certainty and precision. The findings of this section have been represented in Tables 5.23 to 5.29 respectively for the Input, Use and Commodity/Activity-based industry classifications.

Statistical Results with Composite Index : Input-based Classification

The empirical results of the analysis for Input-based classification in terms of composite index of performance are presented in Table 5.23. As the Table shows, of the three industry categories, Metal-based industry performs well on both the dimensions of performance. Agro-based industry scores the highest on PRTF variable, but performance is at the lowest level on GRTH factor. The Chemical-based industry on the contrary turned out to be the poorest on profitability, however, it stands next to the highest level on GRTH factor. The F-ratios indicate that the industries within this classification do not differ significantly from one another on the composite index of performance.

Table 5.23 : ANOVA on Indusry Group and Composite Performance Variables for Input-based Classification of Industries

Industry	Composite Performance Variable				
		GRTH		PRTF	
	No	Mean	SD	Mean	SD
AGRO	51	– 0.11	0.60	0.06	1.20
METAL	23	0.31	1.83	0.02	0.77
CHEMICAL	36	– 0.04	0.64	– 0.10	0.82
OVERALL	110	0.00	1.00	0.00	1.00
F-Ratio		1.50		0.29	

Figures 5.1 and 5.2 depict the comparative performance of different segments of Input-based industry classification for GRTH and PRTF respectively.

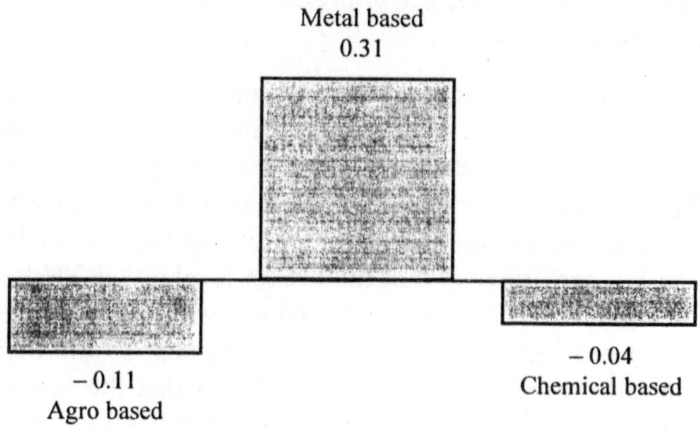

Fig. 5.1: Comparative Growth Performance of Industries : Input-based Classification

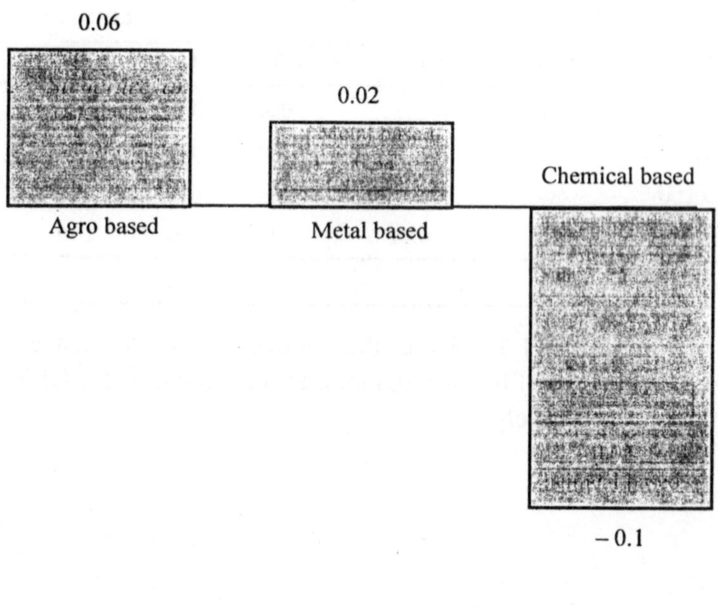

Fig. 5.2: Comparative Profitability Performance of Industries : Input-based Classification

Pairwise Comparison

The HSD value in the Tukey's test of multiple comparison reveals that no industry group is significantly different from the other in any of the pairs on any of the two dimensions of performance, viz. GRTH and PRTF. Table 5.24 below reports the results.

Table 5.24 : Tukey's Test of Multiple Comparison of Industry Performances in Terms of Composite Performance Measures : Input-Based Classification

Performance Variable	Pairs of Comparison*	Difference	HSD (at 5% level)
GRTH	A - M	– 0.43	0.58
	A - C	– 0.07	
	M - C	– 0.35	
PRTF	A - M	0.04	0.59
	A - C	0.17	
	M - C	0.13	

Note: * A, M & C stand for Agro, Metal and Chemical based Industries respectively.

Statistical Results with Composite Index : Use Based Classification

Table 5.25 shows the results of ANOVA on industry group and composite performance indices for Use-based industry classification. Of the four industry categories, Capital goods category is showing the highest growth performance while consumer goods segment is the poorest one. Basic and Intermediate goods segments are good with marginal differences with each other. The results on PRTF factor are rather contrary to that of GRTH. The Consumer goods category has given the best performance to be followed by Capital segment of industry. Basic and Intermediate goods industries are the poorly performing on PRTF factor. The F-ratios indicate that industry segments are statistically and significantly different from one another in respect of only PRTF factor of performance (at 1 per cent level of significance).

Table 5.25 : ANOVA on Industry Group and Composite Performance Variables : Use-Based Classification

Industry		Composite Performance Variable			
		GRTH		PRTF	
	No.	Mean	SD	Mean	SD
Basic	38	0.06	0.63	-0.22	1.13
Intermediate	40	0.04	0.75	-0.33	0.95
Capital	16	0.35	2.41	0.25	0.75
Consumer	58	-0.16	0.64	0.30	0.92
Overall	152	0.00	1.00	0.00	1.00
F-ratio		1.229		4.384[a]	

Note: [a] Significant at 1%.

Figures 5.3 and 5.4 show the comparative performance of different categories of Use-based industry classification on GRTH and PRTF respectively.

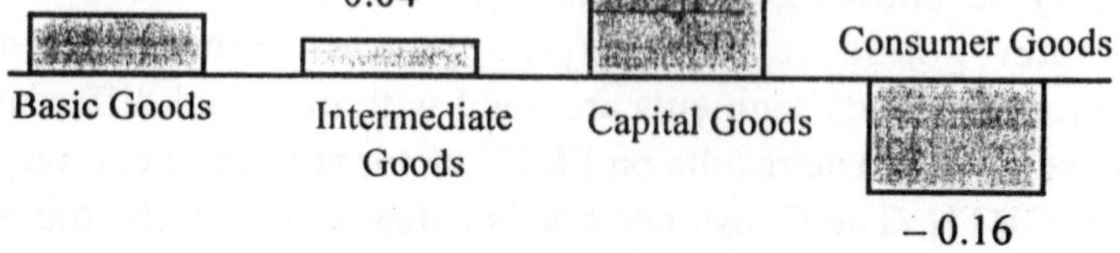

Fig. 5.3: Comparative Growth Performance of Industry : Use Based Classification

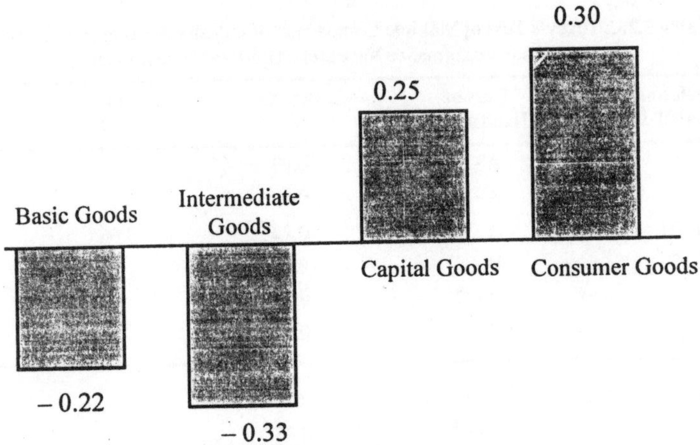

Fig. 5.4: Comparative Profitability Performance of Industries : Use-based Classification

Pairwise Comparison

The Tukey's test of multiple comparison shows that only the difference between the PRTF performance of Consumer and Intermediate segment of industries is significant at 5 per cent level of significance. The profitability performance of Consumer goods industry is significantly higher than that of Intermediate goods industry. Results are shown in Table 5.26.

Statistical Results with Composite Performance : Commodity/ Activity-based Classification

The investigation of Table 5.27 reveals that the mean performance of iron and steel, paint, pharmaceutical, sugar, tyre and tube industries is above the overall mean value of GRTH and PRTF on the contrary, aluminium, cotton textile, jute and paper industries are performing poorly on both the factors of performance. Automobile, cement, man made fibre, electricity, shipping, and vanaspati industries are performing well on only GRTH and inversely, electrical machinery, fertilisers, tea, tobacco, trading as well construction industries are good on only PRTF factor. The results of Table 5.27 are summarised in Table 5.28.

Table 5.26 : Tukey's Text of Multiple Comparison of Industry Performances in Terms of Composite Performance Measures : Use-Based Classification

Performance Variable	Pairs of Comparison*	Difference	HSD (at 5 % level)
	A - B	0.02	
	A - C	– 0.29	
GRTH	A - D	0.22	0.66
	B - C	– 0.31	
	B - D	0.20	
	C - D	0.51	
	A - B	0.11	
	A - C	– 0.47	
PRTF	A - D	– 0.52	0.63
	B - C	– 0.58	
	B - D	– 0.63**	
	C - D	– 0.05	

Note: * A, B, C and D stand respectively for Basic, Intermediate, Capital and Consumer Industries.

** Significant at 5% level.

It can be concluded from the analysis that profitability and growth can be different and sometimes conflicting objectives of a business entity. For example, tea industry ranks first among the 21 industries on profitability factor but the same is performing very poorly on growth factor, ranking sixteenth. Similarly, shipping industry is on the top rank as regarding growth but stands at the seventeenth place in respect of profitability dimension, showing below the overall mean PRTF value.

The null hypothesis of inter-industry performance differences is rejected with fairly high degree of confidence. The F-ratios show the inter-industry differences to be significant at 1 per cent level for GRTH as well as PRTF.

Table 5.27 : ANOVA on Industry Group and Composite Performance Variables for Commodity/Activity Based Industry Classification

Industry		Composite Performance Variable			
		GRTH		PRTF	
	No.	Mean	SD	Mean	SD
Aluminium	4	– 0.40	0.54	– 0.13	0.88
Automobile	10	0.23	0.68	– 0.09	0.73
Cement	10	0.21	0.74	– 0.97	2.06
Cotton Textile	8	– 0.21	0.29	– 0.02	0.49
Elec. Machinery	9	– 0.20	0.61	0.33	0.86
Fertilisers	6	– 0.20	0.49	0.34	0.37
Iron & Steel	10	0.08	0.47	0.01	0.60
Jute	7	– 0.32	0.55	– 1.59	1.20
Man=made Fibre	14	0.13	0.78	– 0.29	0.94
Paints	6	0.06	0.35	0.17	0.55
Paper	10	– 0.52	0.61	– 0.24	0.60
Pharmaceutical	10	-0.06	0.93	0.17	0.62
Sugar	9	0.05	0.48	0.34	0.41
Tea	10	– 0.25	0.55	1.65	1.21
Tobacco	4	– 0.43	0.24	0.26	0.42
Type & Tube	9	0.32	0.99	0.09	0.57
Vanaspati	4	– 0.03	0.86	– 0.09	0.58
Construction	8	– 0.82	0.70	0.01	0.76
Electricity	7	0.15	0.10	– 0.10	0.45
Shipping	6	0.78	0.93	– 0.19	0.43
Trading	10	– 0.24	0.66	0.13	0.43
Overall	171	– 0.07	0.70	– 0.00	1.01
F-Ratios		2.05[a]		4.03[a]	

Note: Significant level : [a] = 1%.

Table 5.28 : Brief view of Industry Performances in Terms of Composite Index : Commodity/Activity-based Classification

Performanace	Industry
Good on Both	Iron and Steel, Paint, Pharmaceutical, Sugar, Tyre and Tube.
Good on GRTH only	Automobile, Cement, Man-made Fibre, Vanaspati, Electricity, Shipping.
Good on PRTF only	Electrical Machinery, Fertilisers, Tea, Tobacco, Construction, Trading.
Poor on Both	Aluminium, Cotton Textile, Jute, Paper.

Figures 5.5 and 5.6 present the comparative performance of different categories of Commodity/Activity-based industry classification on GRTH and PRTF respectively.

The findings of Tukey's test are summarised in Table 5.29 to provide a brief view of the results of pairwise comparison of performances of different industries within Commodity/Activity-based classification of industries.

Table 5.29 : Summary of Findings of Tukey's Test of Multiple Comparison on Composite Performance : Commodity/Activity-based Industry Classification

Performance	Significant Differences Between Means at 5 per cent Level of Significance.
GRTH	Shipping higher than: Construction, Paper.
PRTF	Tea higher than: Jute, Cement, Man-made Fibre, Paper, Shipping, Aluminium, Electricity, Vanaspati, Automobile, Cotton Textile, Construction, Iron and Steel. Jute lower than: Tyre and Tube, Trading, Paint, Pharmaceutical, Tobacco, Electrical Machinery, Fertiliser, Sugar, Tea.

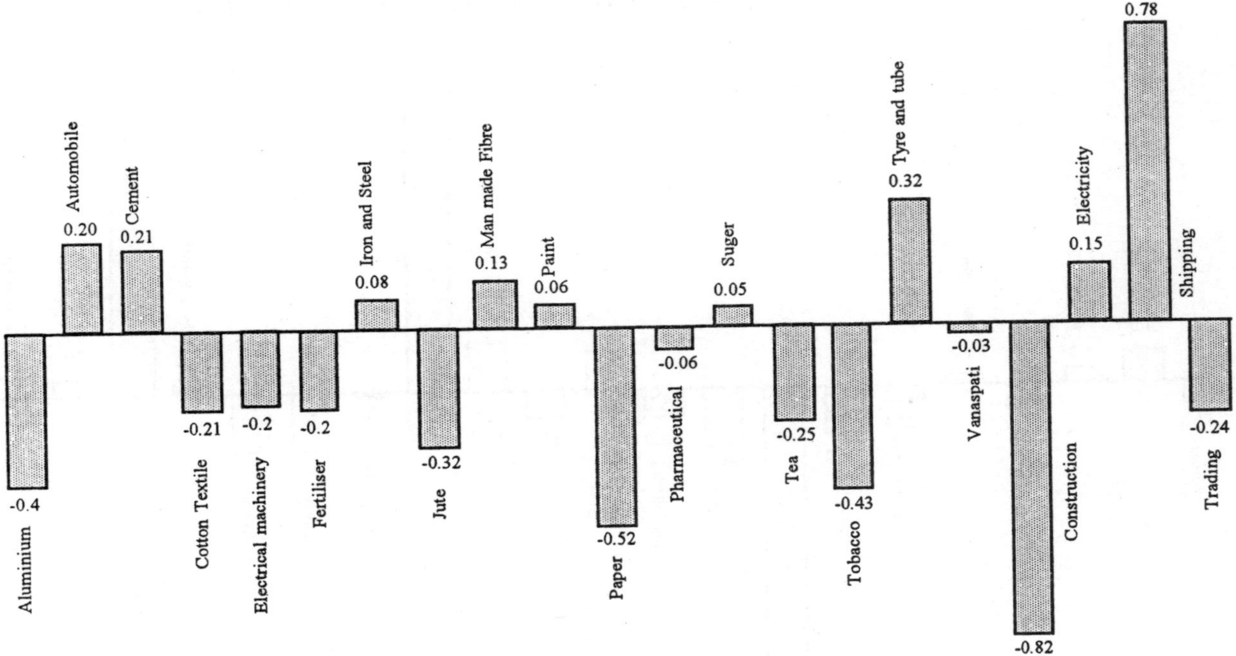

Fig. 5.5: Comparative Growth Performance of Industry : Commodity/Activity Based Classification

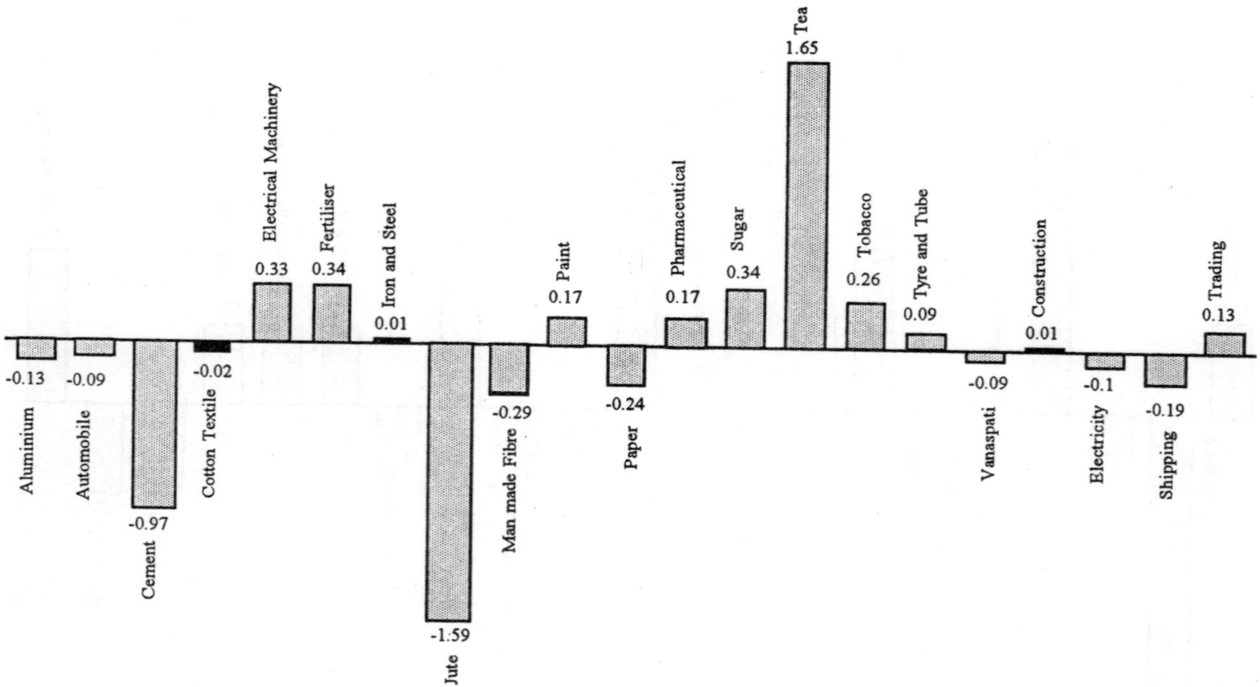

Fig. 5.6: Comparative Growth Performance of Industry : Commodity/Activity Based Classification

Discussion of Results : Input-based Classification

The Agro-based segment is showing the worst performance on GRTH while it ranks the top on PRTF factor of performance. The causes of poor growth performance of this industry group can be attributed to various factors. Many researchers have examined the link between agriculture and industry in India (Ahluwalia, 1985 has provided some references). Our sample of Agro-based group includes companies from tea (10), tobacco (4), cotton (8), jute (7), vanaspati (4), sugar (9), and tyre and tube (9) industries (Figures in brackets show the number of companies in each industry). Agro-based industries are affected adversely by droughts and floods. Table 5.30 below provides information on droughts in India over the period of our study. The availability of agriculture raw materials significantly affects the performance of Agro-based industries. Cotton textile and jute industries, for instance, are dependent on raw cotton and raw jute respectively.

Table 5.30 : Droughts in India : 1980-81 to 1990-91

Year of Drought	Geographical Area Affected by Droughts		Intensity of Drought
	Million Hectares	% of Total Area	
1982	104	31.6	Near severe
1985	95	28.9	Near severe
1986	60	18.3	Moderate
1987	155	47.2	Severe

Source: Extracted from CMIE's India's Agriculture Sector, Sept. 1995.

During Sixth Plan (1980-85) textile industry suffered from prolonged labour unrest, and insufficient demand. The decline in the output of cotton during the Seventh Plan is attributed to drought and attack of pests in certain cotton growing areas (*Economic Survey* 1988-89). This industry also suffered due to capture of its big market share by man-made fibre industry. The share of man-made fibre has been consistently increasing in the consumption pattern of textiles. It is the distinctive qualities of this fibre by virtue of which its consumption increased tremendously over the years. The cotton textile mills have also been facing the problems of replacement of old and obsolete machinery.

The jute industry is the worst in our analysis on performance. This industry faced the problem of sheer shortage of raw materials and the manufacturers have to partly depend on imports. Like cotton industry, this industry has also been facing the problem of old and obsolete machinery for long. Shortage of power and lack of incentives on the part of Government also contributed to the worse condition of the industry. Apart from these, many substitute materials have been introduced like paper and cloth which can be used in place of jute goods safely and effectively.

The condition of sugar industry has been rather comfortable mainly because of the measures initiated by the Government. The ratio of free sale quota has been increased continuously over the period under our study for the betterment of the industry. The Government has increased the Statutory Minimum Price (SMP) for sugarcane in regular intervals in order to improve profitability of the industry. Tea industry is a foreign exchange earning industry and the Government has provided support to this industry in the form of loans and subsidies to boost the production of tea (*Economic Survey* 1990-91).

If both indices of composite performance are taken into consideration, the Metal-based group can be stated to be the best performing segment. This group is ranking top on GRTH factor and is marginally lower than the best performing group on PRTF factor. The constituents of this industry did rather well during Sixth Plan (1980-85). The production of machine tools, passenger cars, motorcycles exceeded the targets during the Sixth Plan. The Government has helped this industry group from time to time by solving its problems, strengthening its competitive position and reducing its cost disadvantages. For example, the budget for 1987-88 revised the tariff rates upward on selected imports from 55 per cent to 85 per cent in order to provide protection to indigenous manufacturers (*Economic Survey* 1987-88, p. 36).

The Chemical-based group stands second on GRTH factor and is at the bottom in case of PRTF. The contents of this group in our study are fertilisers (6), man-made fibre (14), paints (6) and pharmaceuticals (10) industries. The fertiliser and pharmaceutical industries have been subjected to price controls of the Government which is supposed to affect the performance of industries adversely. The production of these two industries has been short of the target production during the Sixth Plan. Fertiliser industry has also suffered from time to time because of power cuts, water shortages, equipment breakdown and non-availability of input materials (*Economic Survey*, 1987-88,1988-89 and other relevant issues). The Government, however, has done certain favours to pharmaceutical industry, e.g. Government has extended the system of delicensing many a times for this industry (*Economic Survey*—various issues). The man-made fibre industry has had a high time and would continue to retain exceeding position. It has captured a big market share from the cotton textile by virtue of its distinctive qualities (discussed above). Paints industry is an intermediate industry. It has been performing well because the industries on which its demand is dependent (e.g. engineering) have been doing well in production. Most of the input materials consumed by paint industry is indigenously available. The import of finished paints has been restricted to a great extent (*Industrial Survey*, SEOD, Dec. 1990).

Discussion of Results : Use-based Classification

The Capital goods sector has played an important role in the industrial development of India over the years and it has come up as a large and diversified sector. In our analysis, the Capital goods segment of Use-based classification of industries is the highest performing segment on growth while the same is ranking second on profitability factor of performance (see Table 5.25). This superiority can be related to the rapid growth of heavy industries during sixties on account of good public investment programmes initiated by positive import substitution policies which increased the share of Capital goods from 11 per cent in 1960-61 to 15 per cent in 1965-66. Moreover, high protection to Capital goods industry had favoured the growth of this group of industries. The import licensing system also supposed to help grow this industry. The results of this segment are also in line with that of *Economic Survey* (1990-91) which provided the group-wise indices of production and annual growth rates of Use-based groups of all industries from 1980-81 to 1989-90. The Capital goods continued to show a high growth rate of over 20 per cent in 1990-91 also (*Economic Survey*, 1990-91, p. 40).

Our sample of capital goods industries consists of companies from electrical machinery, non-electrical machinery and automobile industries. The Sixth Plan (1980-85) sought to provide special attention to the Capital goods industry. The production of machine tools, passenger cars, motorcycles and scooters exceeded the targets in this plan. Further, to boost up the growth and to solve some of the problems faced by the Capital goods sector, the budget for 1987-88 announced certain important reliefs to favour this sector. The tariff rates on project imports were revised upward from 55 per cent to 85 per cent in order to provide protection to indigenous producers and reduce partiality towards imports. The import duty of equipment for electronic industry was revised. Some special measures were also announced for technological upgradation for selected capital goods (*Economic Survey* 1987-88, p.36).

The Basic goods industry is holding second place with more than overall mean performance on growth and it is having the third rank on profitability factor. The constituents of Basic goods industry in our study are fertilisers, cement, iron and steel, aluminium, and electricity industries. The cement industry was subjected to price and distribution controls of the government. But from February 1982, the control on this industry was progressively removed and on 28 February, 1989, the government announced complete decontrol of cement industry. The investment and production in this industry increased substantially since the partial decontrol of cement industry (*Economic Survey* 1988-89,

Annual Plan 1989-90). The Minimum Economic Capacity (MEC) was prescribed for aluminium and fertiliser industries so that the units in these industries could automatically extend their capacity upto this limit and take advantage of scale economies (*Economic Survey*, 1988-89). The poor profitability performance of Basic goods industry can be attributed to power shortages, price and distribution control by the government, and various other problems in respect of cement, fertilisers and aluminium. The electricity generation was also adversely affected by power shortages and monsoon failures (*Economic Survey* 1987-88,1990-91).

Intermediate goods stands third on growth while it is at the bottom on profitability. It consists of tyre and tube (9), man'made fibre (14), vanaspati (4), paint (6) and jute (7). The tyre and tube and paints are good on both the indicators of performance while the jute industry is the poor performing on both the indicators in our analysis. Man-made fibre and vanaspati are showing mixed results. Jute industry could not keep pace with the consistently increasing domestic demand and the volume of jute exports declined over the years (see Table 5.35) and the decline was maximum for the period we studied. This industry had been facing the problem of raw material shortages, power shortages, old and obsolete machinery etc. It also lacked incentives on the part of government. The heavy losses of production and exports of jute are also related to the increased use of synthetic substitutes (*Industrial Survey*, Stock Exchange Official Directory, June 6,1994. No.XXVIII/23). The man-made fibre industry has achieved good growth mainly on account of the distinctive qualities of this fibre and as a result textile consumption trend shifts in favour of this fibre (see Table 5.34). However, man-made fibre industry is very poor on profitability in our analysis. Paint and tyre and tube industries have done well on both the indicators possibly due to the good growth of the industries such as automobiles and engineering on which their demand is dependent.

The Consumer goods group is at the bottom for growth while it holds the highest rank for profitability index. The constituent companies of Consumer goods group belong to paper (10), tobacco

(4), tea (10), cotton textile (8), pharmaceuticals (10), sugar (9), and automobile (7) industries. Sugar, tea, tobacco and cotton textile are agro-based industries. The growth of Agro-based industries is affected adversely by droughts and floods. Table 5.30 gives information on droughts in India during the period under this study. The production of pharmaceuticals and commercial vehicles like that of textile, and sugar fell short of targets during the Sixth Plan (1980-85). But the production of passenger cars, cars and motorcycles exceeded targets during the Sixth Plan. The Seventh Plan (1985-90), however, had sought to encourage the modernisation and technological upgradation in industries like textile and sugar, and specific target of productivity was set up for paper industry. Moreover, the Government had been kind to pharmaceutical industry, e.g. Government extended the system of delicensing many times for this industry (*Economic Survey*—various issues). As a result, the Indian drug industry has made exceptional progress both in terms of range and quantity of production. Consequently, this industry has become self-sufficient in a number of bulk drugs (*Economic Survey,* 1987-88).

Discussion of Results : Commodity/Activity Based Classification

Iron and steel, paints, pharmaceuticals, sugar and tyre and tube industries are showing more than overall mean performance on both the indicators of performance (Table 5.27). Iron and steel are used as basic materials in many industries, e.g. metal products, electrical machinery, transport equipment, textile and other machinery. This is a power based and highly capital intensive industry. Steel casting is an essential input for all engineering industries and the growth of this industry is closely related to the growth of the engineering industry This industry has been, by and large, in the hands of State, which has provided a very controlled environment to this industry. The industry has been protected from external markets by making a very restrictive import policy. This industry needs huge investments and has a long gestation period and is highly dependent on infrastructure supply. This industry has got some privileges. Rich iron ore mines are found here and coal and iron are available in close proximity. Moreover, this industry is self-sufficient as regarding technological aspect and is able to export technological know how to the developing countries. The required machinery is indigenously available. The latest international techniques are being used to carry the work of welding in this industry. There is a Joint Plant Committee (JPC) which revises the prices of iron and steel items from time to time in order to neutralise the rise in the cost of inputs like coal, power, railways freights. Minimum Economic Capacity (MEC) was announced for steel industry so that it could itself expand the capacity upto the prescribed MEC level. Contrary to the stagnation in the late sixties and the seventies, this industry improved much during eighties as regarding capacity utilisation and technological innovation. Production increased while energy consumption declined considerably. Even the companies which were in loss since long, generated profits. The changes also took place in respect of managerial techniques within this industry. During the late eighties, the capacity utilisation reached 90 per cent.

Paints play important role to preserve and protect all types of architectural structures, metal and wooden things from the odds of weather. Paints are extensively used in light engineering, electrical and chemical industries. Pigments (organic and inorganic), synthetic resins and industrial solvents are the main materials used in the manufacturing of paints. Most of the input materials are available indigenously. The import of finished paints has been restricted to a great extent. Paints is an intermediate industry. Its growth and expansion is closely linked with the growth and expansion of different engineering, chemical and other paints consuming industries. During the period of our study demand of paints has increased due to the growth and expansion of industries on which its demand depends.

The Indian paint industry is capable to meet the requirement of industries like transport, chemical, light engineering, electrical industries (*Industrial Survey*, SEOD, December1986). The equipment and machinery used in manufacturing paints is mostly available indigenously. Some companies have also been exporting paints to other countries, e.g. USSR, Middle East countries, Bangladesh. But, there has been dearth of technological innovations in this industry. The Government has, however, helped this industry to adopt new techniques to produce sophisticated, qualitative and durable paints to meet the requirements of developing and growing industries (*Industrial Survey*, SEOD, December 1990).

The Indian pharmaceutical industry has achieved an excellent growth both in terms of quantity and range of production, and resultantly it has become self-sufficient in bulk of drugs. The Government has prescribed Minimum Economic Scales of production in respect of certain drugs so that manufacturers in this industry could take benefits of economies of scale. The delicensing has also been extended from time to time to this industry. The Government announced Drug Price Control Order in August 1987 in order to encourage production in desired areas. In March 1985, the Government announced the delicensing of 25 broad categories of industries. In June 1985, delicensing was extended to 82 bulk drugs and related drug formulations (*Economic Survey*, 1985-86, p. 29). As in the case of electrical fans and equipment, automobile, tyre and tube, and cement industry, the facility of broad banding was extended to this industry also so that manufactures could adjust the product mix in line with changing market conditions and utilise their capacity to the optimum level (Economic Survey 1986-89, p.47). The production of this industry was lower than the target during Sixth Plan. This industry also faced the price control of the Government which has an unfavourable impact on the growth of the industry. Moreover, the production of drugs and pharmaceuticals fell short of target during Sixth Plan (1980-85).

Sugar is an important export commodity in India and it has emerged as the major foreign exchange earning commodity in the country. The production of sugar and sugarcane have been quite comfortable since 1980-81. This is evident from the Table 5.31. The sugar is an agro-based industry and irregular trend in the production of sugar can be attributed mainly to natural calamities such as droughts, late rains etc. The industry is also effected on account of diversion of sugarcane for the production of *gur* and *khandsari*.

Table 5.31 : Production of Sugarcane

(In million tonnes)

Year	Production
1980-81	154.2
1985-86	170.7
1986-87	186.1
1987-88	196.7
1988-89	203.0
1989-90	225.6
1990-91	240.3

Source: Statistical Profile of the Indian Economy, Stock Exchange Official Directory, 3rd August 1992 No.XXVI/30(1/2).

The rising trend in cane production is supposed to be the outcome of various policy measures undertaken by the Government and development efforts initiated by the sugar industry as well as by the cane growers. To make the cane cultivation more profitable, the Statutory Minimum Price (SMP) for sugarcane has been revised upward in regular intervals, e.g. the prices per quintal were Rs. 19.50 in 1988-89, Rs. 22 in 1989-90 and Rs. 23 for 1990-91 season. Similarly, the Government increased the free sale quota successively over the period under our study for the betterment of industry, e.g. in 1990-91 the free sale quota was 75 per cent as against 55 per cent of sugar production during October 1, 1990 to November 15, 1990 (*Economic Survey*, 1990-91). Besides these, during the Seventh Plan (1985-90), sugar factories were given loans from Sugar Development Funds for the improvement of cane cultivation, and also for modernisation and expansion of mills (*Economic Survey*, 1988-89). To overcome the difficulties, the Government also announced incentives for the new and expanding sugar factories in terms of excise duty concessions (*Industrial Survey*, SEOD, December 1986). However, the production of sugar was short of targets during the Sixth Plan (1980-85) and the Seventh Plan (1985-90) had sought to encourage the modernisation and technological upgradation of this industry.

The tyre industry is the major consumer of natural and synthetic rubber. It consumes around 55 per cent of the total production of rubber. The consumption of rubber has increased over the years mainly on account of the growth of the automobile and the road transport industry. The gap between domestic demand and supply is normally bridged through imports. Around 31700 tonnes rubber was imported in 1990-91 as against 26500 tonnès in 1989-90 (*Industrial Survey*, SEOD, January 1993). Almost all the major tyre companies have technological collaboration with the foreign tyre companies and quality has been improved to the international standards. From about a decade back, nylon has taken the place of rayon tyre yarn which has improved the strength and life of tyre. The input material mix up has also been replaced with better make-up to produce better performing tyres. The production in this industry has increased continuously. Production of auto tyres (in Nos.) in 1984 was 109,95,098, in 1985 123,02,905 and in 1986 it increased to 128,53,313. The production increased in 1988-89, 1989-90 and 1990-91 also. Minimum Economic Capacity (MEC) was prescribed for this industry and factories in this industry were able to expand their capacities themselves upto the minimum prescribed limit (*Economic Survey* 1988-89, p.46). Like many other industries this industry was also provided the facility of broad banding. This facility enabled the manufacturer not only to form a product mix according to the dynamic market environment but also facilitated the utilisation of installed capacity to the optimum level (*Economic Survey*, 1988-89, p.47).

Aluminium, cotton textile, jute and paper industries in our analysis are the poorest performing industries. All these industries are performing below the overall mean performance on both the indicators of performance.

The installed capacity of primary aluminium, if fully utilised, has been sufficient to meet the demand of aluminium in the country. But the installed capacity could not be utilised fully mainly on account of inadequate and abrupt supply of power.

Hence India has been importing aluminium to meet the requirements of the country. The following Table provides the information on import of aluminium for 5 years, i.e. from 1983-84 to 1987-88. The main constraint in the production of aluminium has been the shortage of power. The aluminium industry has also been subjected to price control of Government. The Government, however, has made efforts to improve the condition of this industry. Minimum Economic Capacity (MEC) was prescribed for this industry. Bauxite is the principal ore for aluminium production and India has large deposits of this mineral, ranking fifth in the world, next to Australia, Guinea, Brazil and Jamaica. The Government has been making efforts to replace wood and other scarce metals with aluminium. Aluminium has certain distinct qualities, e.g. light weight, high strength-to-weight ratio, non-corrosivity and conductivity. In spite of the promotional efforts by the Government, this industry could not be improved.

Table 5.32 : Imports of Aluminium

Year	Quantity in Tonnes
1983-84	13,000
1984-85	56,000
1985-86	25,055
1986-87	65,000
1987-88 (Estimated)	70,000

Source: *Industrial Survey*, SEOD, 24th June, 1991, No. XXV/25 (2/4).

Textile industry is the most important industry in India in terms of employment and production of export goods. This industry contributed 20 per cent to the total industrial output and accounts for around 30 per cent of the total value of exports. It gives employment to 20 million people. The textile industry of India is mainly cotton based, nearly 70 per cent of the raw material consumed in this industry is cotton. Table 5.33 shows that production of cotton has not been consistent over the period of our study.

Table 5.33 : Production of Cotton

(*in million bales*)

Year	Production
1980-81	7.0
1985-86	8.7
1986-87	6.9
1987-88	6.4
1988-89	8.7
1989-90	11.4
1990-91	9.8

Source: Statistical Profile of the Indian Economy, Stock Exchange Official Directory, 3rd August, 1992, No. XXVI/30 (1/2).

The production of textiles was short of targets during the Sixth Plan (1980-85). During the Sixth Plan textile industry has suffered from prolonged labour unrest and insufficient demand. The Seventh Plan (1985-90) sought to encourage the modernisation and technological upgradation of textile industry. The production target for the Seventh Five Year Plan was achieved easily. The decline in the output of cotton during a few years of Seventh Plan is attributed to drought and spread of pests in certain cotton growing areas. There are many factors which affected the textile industry adversely. The capacity utilisation in this industry is low mainly on account of old and obsolete machinery. This has lowered productivity. The normal working life of the textile machinery is generally 25 years but most of the machinery in use in this industry is more than 50 years old. The cotton textile industry has also been facing the problem of inadequate supply of raw materials and power. The prices of raw materials fluctuated oddly. There are a large number of varieties of cotton in India and this is considered a bottleneck in the progress of this industry. The Government of India held a seminar in the office of Textile Commissioner in July 1987 for reduction of varieties of cotton (*Industrial Survey*, SEOD, 'October 1989, September 1990).

Table 5.34 : Per Capita Availability of Cloth

(In metres)

Period	Cotton cloth	Man-made Fibres	Total
1960-61	13.8	1.2	15.0
1970-71	13.6	2.0	15.6
1980-81	11.0	3.7	14.7
1990-91	15.1	9.0	24.1
1992-93	15.6	8.0	23.7

Source: Compiled from *Economic Survey*, 1993-94.

The cotton textile industry has also suffered due to capture of its big market share by man-made fibre industry. The man-made fibre is consistently increasing in the consumption pattern of textiles. Table 5.34 provides information on the consumption pattern of textiles over the years and reveals that it has undergone a sea change. It is the distinctive qualities of man-made fibre by virtue of which its consumption increased tremendously over the years. This fibre is comparatively dearer but has a much longer life. Moreover, it is easier to wash and iron. Besides, it reduces the maintenance cost considerably. The Indian cotton industry has also been facing increasing competition in world markets. This is largely due to low productivity and high cost and consequently high prices of Indian cotton textiles. All these factors contributed to the low profitability and growth of this industry.

India manufactures the largest quantity of jute goods in the world. The jute industry plays an important role in the economy of eastern and north-eastern regions of the country. This industry is the poorest in our analysis on both the dimensions of performance, viz. growth and profitability. This industry has suffered to a great extent in the export market on account of severe competition from other jute producing countries as well as due to introduction of synthetic substitutes. Table 5.35 shows that the exports of jute textiles declined continuously. The jute industry has failed on domestic markets and export fronts because of the introduction of many substitute materials such as paper, cloth and man-made fibre which can be used in place of jute goods safely and effectively.

Table 5.35 : Production, Export and Consumption of Jute Textiles

('000 tonnes)

Year	Production	Exports	Consumption
1950-51	890	790	120
1960-61	1,000	760	280
1970-71	1,090	640	480
1980-81	1,390	440	920
1990-91	1,430	220	1,230
1992-93	1,310	210	1,100

Source: RBI, Report on Currency and Finance, 1992-93 (and previous issues). *Economic Survey*, 1993-94.

It is a well known fact that jute industry is facing a crisis of acute shortage of raw jute since the partition of the country and the manufacturers in this industry have to partly depend on imports. At the time of partition, jute mills remained in India, whereas a major portion of jute producing area went over to Pakistan (later separated as Bangladesh). Even though India is the largest producer of raw jute in the world its production is not enough even to meet fully the needs of the country and consequently exports are also decreasing consistently over the years. Table 5.35 shows that domestic consumptions of jute textiles was increasing consistently over the years as a result of better agricultural produce*.

The production of jute was short of targets during the Sixth Plan (1980-85). Table 5.36 reveals that production of jute has been very inconsistent over the period under study. Production of Jute textiles increased to 13.87 lakh tonnes during 1988-89 as against 11.92 lakh tonnes during 1987-88. This increase was due to the good demand of jute bags for sacking in cement, sugar, fertiliser, and other industries (this demand was improved following the order by Supreme Court in May 1988 on jute

* The demand of jute products has increased mainly on account of development of agriculture and industries in the world. Jute bags had been in great demand for sacking agricultural and industrial products such as wheat, rice, gram, maize, pulses, sugar, fertilisers, cement etc.

packaging reservation). The Government has made many efforts to improve this industry, e.g. the Government made, the Jute Packaging Material (Compulsory use in Packing Commodity) Act, 1987, customs duty on imports of specified items of jute mills machinery had been waived. The Government also created various funds to provide assistance for the improvement of this industry. Like cotton industry, the jute industry is also suffering on account of the problem of old and obsolete machinery, lack of incentives on the part of Government, shortage of power, managerial deficiencies, labour unrest etc.

Table 5.36 : Production of Jute

(In million bales)

Year	Production
1980-81	6.5
1985-86	10.9
1986-87	7.4
1987-88	5.8
1988-89	6.7
1989-90	7.1
1990-91	7.8

Source: Statisical Profile of the Indian Economy, *Stock Exchange Official Directory*, 3rd August, 1992, No.XXVI/30(1/2).

Paper industry is more than a century old. Paper and paper board is manufactured from pulp of wood/other raw materials such as agricultural residue, bagasse etc. India is self-sufficient in the production of most varieties of paper and paper boards and only a few varieties are imported. This industry is facing many problems which can be held responsible for the poor performance of this industry. This is a capital intensive industry and huge investment is needed to set up a large integrated paper mill. Large paper mills consume bamboo and tropical hardwoods and they have been facing the acute shortage of raw materials and ever increasing royalty rates. Furthermore, rise in the prices of coal and power, and inadequate supply of these two inputs have hit the manufacturers badly. The industry is also facing the problem of industrial disputes, financial problems etc. Majority of paper mills still use outdated technology and machinery. 50 years old plants need urgent modernisations and replacement. The Government has taken up various steps to improve the productivity and solve the financial problems of this industry, such as liberalising imports of raw materials, concession in excise duty, broad banding, delicensing etc. Minimum Economic Capacity (MEC) level was prescribed for this industry resultantly the units in this industry were automatically allowed to expand their capacities upto MEC limits.

Automobile, cement, man-made fibre, vanaspati, electricity, and shipping industries are performing above overall mean performance in respect of only GRTH. Production of passenger cars, motorcycles and scooters exceeded the targets during the Sixth Plan (1980-85). The automobile industry has shown steady growth in the early eighties but it crept into recession after August 1990. A growth of 7 per cent was projected for 1990-91 as against 5 per cent growth in 1989-90. The factors which are held responsible for decline of this industry are—sharp rise in the prices of petroleum products, import restrictions, change in depreciation laws, fall in the value of rupee etc. Growth and production of cement industry were affected badly mainly on account of power shortage and labour unrest in some cement plants. However, the investment and production in the industry went up considerably since the partial decontrol of cement in February 1982. The industry was also provided the facility of broad-banding so that the units therein could optimise their capacity utilisation and adjust their product mix according to the dynamic market environment. The Government announced complete decontrol of cement industry with effect from 28th February, 1989. Until then, the Government pursued the policy of price and distribution controls on cement partially (Annual Plan 1989-90, Government of India, Planning Commission, p. 209). The cement industry has recorded continuous growth since planning started. This is evident from Table 5.37 below. Despite the phenomenal growth in this industry, its profitability rank in our study is 20th, the poorest. The bad profitability performance may be attributed to the rise of cost of production, power shortage, partial price and supply control by the Government.

Table 5.37 : Performance of Cement Industry

Year	Installed capacity	Production *(million tonnes)*	Production as a percentage of capacity
1950-51	3.3	2.7	82
1960-61	9.4	7.9	85
1970-71	17.3	14.3	83
1980-81	27.0	18.1	67
1990-91	64.0	48.8	76
1992-93	67.8	54.1	80

Source: RBI, Report on Currency and Finance, 1992-93, Vol. I (various other issues).

The consumption pattern of textiles has undergone a sea change. Table 5.44 evidences the shifting trend of textile consumption over the years. The share of man-made fibre has increased consistently in the consumption pattern of textiles. In other words, man-made fibre industry has captured a big market share from cotton textile industry mainly on account of its distinctive qualities such as cost effective maintenance, greater longevity and easier washability and ironing. As regards man-made fibre, while maintaining the dominant position of cotton as main fibre, the Government decided to encourage the use of man-made fibres in different sectors of the industry in the light of increase in domestic and international consumption and for this purpose, the Government increased the availability of man-made fibre (*Industrial Survey*, SEOD, October 1989 and September 1990).

Historically, India has made efforts to achieve self-sufficiency in food and she has been producing surplus quantities of food. Only after the attainment of sufficient quantities of food, energies are diverted to progress in other areas. In India, need for food processing was realised after the start of Green Revolution. The demand for processed foods has been increasing, both in developed and developing countries, mainly due to the changing lifestyles of people and more and more women accepting jobs out of house. Processed food now accounts for over 50 per cent of the diet in many developed countries. Minimum Economic Capacity (MEC) was prescribed for this industry also.

Electricity is listed in the concurrent list of Constitution and hence development of the power sector is the joint responsibility of Central and State governments. Around two-thirds of the power generating capacity in the country is in the hands of State governments. The private sector owns only nominal share of the total power generating capacity. We could find only 7 companies according to our sample formation process in the private sector. Adequate, timely and reliable supply of electricity plays a critical role in the development of agriculture industry and other sectors of the economy. The demand for electricity will go on increasing as far as the development is desired in the field of agriculture, industry and other sectors.

Power generation increased at the rate of 9.2 per cent per annum during the eighties (*Industrial Survey*, 1988-89, p. 30). Table 5.38 provides information on the installed capacity and generation of electricity. There is steady growth in installed capacity and generation of electricity over our study period. However, the achievement of hydel generation was sometimes less than target which could be attributed to insufficient or late monsoon resulting in reduced inflows in the reservoirs. Consequently some hydel stations were forced to close. The overall satisfactory performance of power generation might be possible mainly on account of progressive increase in the Plant Load Factor (PLF*) of thermal power stations (*Economic Survey*, 1987-88, p.22).

---

* Plant Load Factor (PLF) is defined as actual energy produced by a thermal power plant during a period as a percentage of the maximum energy that could have been produced, had the plant generated at full capacity during the same period

Table 5.38 : Electricity—Installed Capacity and Generation

Year	Installed Capacity (Bn.Kw)	Generation (Mn.Kw.)
1980-81	33.3	119.3
1983-84	43.7	151.0
1984-85	47.4	169.2
1985-86	52.3	183.4
1986-87	55.0	203.3
1987-88	60.5	219.0
1988-89	65.5	241.3
1989-90	71.8	268.4
1990-91	74.4	288.7

Source: Statistical Profile of the Indian Economy, *Stock Exchange Official Directory*, 3rd August, 1992, No.XXVI/30(1/2).

Shipping industry is number one on growth but it failed badly on profitability. Table 5.39 depicts the growth of shipping tonnage for our period of study. The shipping industry has suffered due to foreign exchange crisis as well as gulf crisis on the shipping world. The Indian shipping scene improved in 1990-91 with the boom in the world shipping. The performance of shipping had been bad during the Seventh Plan. The shipping tonnage declined from 6.32 million GRT in Sixth Plan to 5.98 million GRT in Seventh Five Year Plan. The factors which are held responsible for this decline are the increased rate of scrapping of vessels and weak freight market. The Indian shipping industry also suffered due to the old ships, the inadequate containerisation and specialised vessels, absence of requisite handling capacity at the port and competition from the foreign companies.

Table 5.39 : Growth of Shipping Tonnage

Period	Gross Registered Tonnage (*Million*)
At the end of Sixth Plan (March 1985)	6.32
At the end of Seventh Plan (March 1990)	5.98
March end 1991	6.03

Source: *Economic Outlook*, CMIE, June 1992, p. 39.

Electrical machinery, fertilisers, tea, tobacco, construction and trading industries have done well on PRTF only with above overall mean performance. All these are showing less than overall mean performance on GRTH factor of performance. Electrical machinery is an import intensive industry and its growth is affected adversely because of import restriction. Some segments of this industry (e.g. electric motor industry) are well established in the country and has good demand within the country. The capacity utilisation in electric motor industry has been around 80 per cent. The plant, machinery and spares for the production of electrical fans, by and large, are indigenously available. Most of the raw material consumed in electrical machinery industry is also indigenously available (Industrial Survey, SEOD, October 1990). This industry contributed the maximum to the decline among the manufacturing industries. However, this industry had been benefited the most from the liberalised industrial and trade policies during the eighties (*Economic Outlook*, CMIE, June 1992).

Fertiliser is an important input for higher agricultural produce and it has been given high priority by the Government. The agricultural output can be increased by applying fertilisers, improved method of cultivation and high yielding seeds as the agricultural land is limited. The production of fertilisers was short of targets during the Sixth Plan (1980-85) and the Seventh Plan (1985-90) set up specific targets for this industry. Presently, indigenous production of fertilisers is not sufficient to meet the demand of the country and fertilisers have to be imported to supply the needs of the country. This industry has been facing a number of problems such as shortage of power, water, natural gas and imported phosphoric acid. It has also suffered due to equipment failure, labour unrest and demand constraints because of droughts. This industry has also been subjected to price control of the Government which effects the growth of the industry adversely. In view of the importance of fertilisers, fertiliser industry has been receiving a variety of subsidies from the Government since 1977. The quantities of subsidy has gone up year after year, from Rs. 375 crores in 1981-82 to Rs. 4389 crores in 1990-91 (Report on Currency and Finance 1992-93). The future of this industry does not seem certain because of rising production costs, shortage of input materials, erratic pricing and subsidy policies. No new company has come up in this industry from 1986 onwards.

India is the world's largest producer of tea. This is one of the oldest and well organised industries in India. This industry has a unique position in our national economy. This is an agro-based and export oriented industry and is situated in backward areas (Reserve Bank of India, 1981, *Economic Survey*, SEOD, July 1995). Tea is grown in an area of over 4 lakh hectares. It is one of the most labour intensive industries. Table 5.40 gives data on production of tea. The production of tea has not shown any good rise. The increase in the demand of tea from within the country has been higher than the increase in production, this resulted in a decline in exportable surplus of tea (*Economic Survey,* 1993-94).

Table 5.40 : Production of Tea

(In million tonnes)

Year	Production
1980-81	0.6
1985-86	0.7
1986-87	0.6
1987-88	0.7
1988-89	0.7
1989-90	0.7*

* Provisional.

Source : Statistical profile of the Indian Economy, SEOD, 3rd August, 1992, No. XXVI/ 30 (1/2).

The Government has been making continuous efforts to increase tea exports through fiscal and financial incentives. The exporters of tea also received support from Brand Promotion Fund Scheme in the form of interest free loan (*Economic Survey* 1990-91).Tea exports during 1990-91 amounted to 199.5 million kgs. worth Rs. 1045.4 crores as against 211.8 million kgs. worth Rs. 914.8 crores in 1989-90. The tea was exported to USSR, United Kingdom, Iran and ARE (Arab Republic of Egypt). During the year 1990-91, the tea industry received help in the form of replantation subsidy, tea area rejuvenative and consolidation subsidy, the hire-purchase for machinery and equipment etc. (Industrial Survey, SEOD, December 1992; Report on Currency and Finance, 1990-91, Vol. I, RBI). Tobacco industry is also an important industry. It brings foreign exchange to the country. This is an agro-based industry and suffered on account of droughts (*Economic Survey,* 1987-88, p. 31). We could not find literature on tobacco, construction and trading industries from various sources. Therefore, we are not in a position to relate the results of these industries to the economic attributes.

Conclusion

This is the major chapter of this book which tests the hypothesis of inter-industry performance differentials. Estimations are based on the data of 187 companies which have been classified into three samples representing three different industry classification systems. The three industry classifications for which analysis has been carried out are—Input-based classification, Use-based classification and Commodity/Activity-based classification. Performance has been operationalised in terms of profitability and growth dimensions. Return on Equity (ROE) and Return on Assets (ROA) have been taken to represent profitability while Growth in Sales (GSALES), Growth in Total Net Assets

(GNTA) and Growth in Dividend (GDIV) have represented growth.

ANOVA has been carried out to test the hypothesis of inter-industry performance variations. The analysis has been carried out, firstly, on five performance indicators separately and later on, the information on the five performance indicators have been condensed through Factor Analysis which produced two composite indices, namely growth and profitability. The analysis carried out at first stage has been repeated on the composite index of performance. At the first stage of analysis, null hypothesis of inter-industry performance differences has been rejected for only GSALES and GTNA indicators of performance in case of Input-based classification of industry while only ROA indicator has showed the inter-industry performance differences to be significant for Use-based industry classification. However, for Commodity/ Activity-based industry classification, ROA, GTNA and GDIV measures of performance have rejected the null hypothesis of inter-industry performance differentials at a high degree of confidence.

At second stage when the results are taken on composite index of performance, no group has differed significantly from one another on any of the two composite indices of performance for Input-based industry classification, while in case of Use-based classification, inter-industry performance differentials have been found highly significant for only profitability (PRTF) dimension of performance. However, segments of Commodity/ Activity-based classification have differed significantly from one another on both the indices of performance, viz. growth (GRTH) and profitability (PRTF).

Empirical analysis has been followed by discussion of results which has sought to relate inter-industry differences in performance to certain attributes of Indian economy. It has been seen that certain industry groups are endowed with some favours which may be economic, political, climatic or structural resulting in their superiority of performance. The industries may suffer as well due to these factors, for example, agro-based industries are affected adversely by droughts, floods and non-availability of agricultural raw materials.

6

INDUSTRY EFFECTS, FIRM CHARACTERISTICS AND PERFORMANCE

Introduction

The last chapter has revealed that, by and large, inter-industry differences do exist and are statistically significant. We have also sought to relate such differences to certain attributes of Indian economy. There are, however, number of other factors which have been shown to have an impact on performance, like size, leverage, risk, age, skill, capital intensity and market share of the firm. In this chapter, we have examined the role of industry membership along with various other variables in explaining the performance variations of firms. OLS regression models have been used to disintegrate performance variations. Composite index of performance constructed with the help of factor analysis is used as dependent variable whereas six firm characteristic variables have been employed as the determinants of performance in multiple regression models. Industry effects have been isolated by employing dummy variables in the models.

Sample

The samples and period of study for the three different industry classifications to be analysed in this chapter are the same as were used for the analysis on composite index of performance in Chapter 5. The 11-year period of study is 1980-81 to 1990-91. The Commodity/Activity-based industry classification contains 171 companies spread over 21 industries. The Use-based industry classification consists of 152 companies categorised into four groups of industries. There are 110 companies in Input-based industry classification divided into three industry groups. Table 6.1 sets out the detailed break-up of samples for the three industry classification to be examined in this chapter.

Table 6.1 : Make up of Sample for Analysis of Firm and Industry: Effects on Performance

Industry Group	Number of Companies
Commodity/Activity Based Classification	
1. Aluminium	4
2. Automobile	10
3. Cement	10
4. Cotton Textile	8
5. Electrical Machinery	9
6. Fertiliser	6
7. Iron and Steel	10
8. Jute	7
9. Man-made Fibre	14
10. Paint	6
11. Paper	10
12. Pharmaceutical	10
13. Sugar	9
14. Tea	10
15. Tobacco	4
16. Tyre and Tube	9
17. Vanaspati	4
18. Construction	8
19. Electricity	7
20. Shipping	6
21. Trading	10
Total	171
Used Based Classification	
1. Basic Goods	38
2. Intermediate Goods	40
3. Capital Goods	16
4. Consumer Goods	58
Total	152
Input-based Classification	
1. Agro-based	51
2. Metal-based	23
3. Chemical-based	36
Total	110

Performance

The definition and concept of performance is the same as was used for analysis on composite index of performance in Chapter 5. The performance has been defined in terms of profitability and growth. Return on Equity (ROE) and Return on Assets (ROA) have been taken to represent profitability. Growth in Sales (GSALES), Growth in Total Net Assets (GTNA) and Growth in Dividend (GDIV) indicate growth aspect of performance. Two factors were extracted by factor analysing the above five performance indicators (The results are provided in Tables 5.8 to 5.22 in Chapter 5). These two factors have been named as GRTH (growth) and PRTF (profitability) on the basis of their concentration around the performance indicators.

Hypotheses and Variables

Industry Effects

As mentioned earlier, industry characteristics have vital concern in the analysis of firm performance. Rumelt (1982) investigated the importance of industry in explaining firm profitability. He identified that industry effects were primarily responsible for the high performance of 'related constrained' firms. Many other researchers have also found that industry characteristics play an important role in the analysis of company performance. Schmalensee (1985) found industry effects to be the major source of the cross-sectional variance of profitability. Firm effects were insignificant in his study. Scott and Pascoe's (1986) results showed that both, firm and industry effects were important in explaining cross-sectional variations in profitability. Amato and Wilder (1990) used the methodology similar to Schmalensee, and Scott and Pascoe to study the impact of firm and industry effects on rate of return on assets. Industry effects showed up to be the main determinant of rate of return in their model. The adjusted R^2 reduced considerably when industry effects were deleted from the model. Hamilton and Shergill (1993) in their study on strategy, structure and performance of New Zealand quoted companies revealed that industry effects were the strongest in explaining variation in company profitability. Like Schmalensee, Scott and Pascoe, Amato and Wilder, and Hamilton and Shergill, we have employed dummy variables in the models to capture industry effects.

Size

The big firms have been considered to be endowed with certain advantages such as lower costs and higher returns on account of access to capital market (Hall and Weiss, 1967) and economies of scale (Montgomery, 1979; Sidhu and Bhatia, 1993).* Hence, generally a positive hypothesis is set for size-performance relationship.

The size-performance relationship is more likely to be curvi-linear and after reaching a certain stage, the advantage of scale economies may cease and beyond that the relationship may even reverse due to the problems of large scale. Due to the expected curvi-linear size-performance relationship, size variable is generally employed in log form. Therefore, in line with various researchers, we have employed in this study the log of total assets as the measure of size (e.g. Siddharthan and Dasgupta, 1983; Amato and Wilder, 1990; Hamilton and Shergill, 1993). On the basis of economic theory, we expect a positive relationship between size and performance.

Risk

Although economists and researchers in strategic management have great interest in the relationship between risk and profits, not many studies have sought to quantify this relationship (Fisher and Hall, 1969 provide list of references). From some recent past, risk has been prevalent as an important variable in strategic management literature (Bettis, 1981; Bettis and Hall, 1982). Mixed results have been produced on this variable by cross-section

---

* However, mixed evidences have been found on the relationship between firm size and profitability. Schmalensee (1989) provides long list of references.

studies of profitability.* Risk has been taken to denote some degree of hazard which can result on account of various factors such as short-term fluctuations in profits, changes in consumer tastes, changes in technology, changes in Government policy, strategic moves of competitors (Bettis, 1981). Entrepreneurs have to make decisions in the face of uncertainty about future events and they cannot predict future events with complete certainty. As such risk can be measured as the difference of the actual outcome with the anticipated outcome (Fisher and Hall, 1969). Due to importance of risk and the mixed nature of the evidence in respect of the relationship between risk and returns, a risk variable was included in this study. In line with Hamilton and Shergill (1993) we have incorporated the coefficient of variation of Earnings Per Share (EPS) over the period 1981 to 1991 as measure of risk. Since investors usually require a higher rate of return for undertaking riskier projects, we expect a positive association between risk and performance.

Leverage

Leverage has been employed widely in the studies of performance (Hall and Weiss, 1967; Harris, 1986; Scott and Pascoe, 1986; Pant, 1991; Hamilton and Shergill, 1993; Sidhu and Bhatia, 1993). The decision as to the capital structure or leverage of a company is a significant managerial decision which reflects management's choice between shareholders' return and risk. The effect of leverage may be favourable or unfavourable. It will magnify shareholders' earnings when the cost of debt is lower than the company's rate of return. However, the leverage happens to be unfavourable when the rate of return on the company's assets is lower than the cost of debt capital. We assume that mostly the firms will venture to borrow capital when they expect that they will be able to earn more than the cost of debt capital and hence

* For instance, Bothwell, Cooley and Hall (1984) and Hirschey (1985) found a weak relationship between risk and profitability. On the contrary, Neumann, Bobel and Haid (1985), Harris (1986), and Hamilton and Shergill (1993) found differences in risk to be very strong.

a positive relationship between leverage and performance.

We have used the following formula to compute leverage variable:

$$\text{Leverage} = \frac{\text{Total Long Term Debts}}{\text{Shareholders' Funds}} \times 100$$

The leverage or the ratio between debt and equity indicates the proportion between shareholders' funds and the total long term borrowed capital. In other words, it indicates owner's stake in business. As regards preference share, the Controller of Capital Issue treats redeemable preference shares (which are to be redeemed in 12 years or less) as part of debt. As our study tends to find the impact of leverage on financial and growth performance, preference capital has been included in debt. The preference divided is fixed like the interest cost and the common shareholders' earnings will be magnified if the rate of preference divided is less than the firm's overall rate of return. So far as the risk is concerned, we have employed a separate measure to capture the impact of risk on performance.

Skill

From some time back, importance of human capital is being realised in the field of economic development and growth. Salary, status, power and security of the personnel employed in the company have been considered to have linkage with corporate growth (Barna, 1962; Penrose, 1959). Various researchers in their studies of performance analysis have postulated positive associations between the skill of the employees and financial performance of the organisation (Siddharthan and Dasgupta, 1983; Kumar, 1985). Caves (1974) considered the high skill levels of firms' employees in the industry to be an important source of monopolistic advantage. Siddharthan and Dasgupta (1983) found the differences in skill levels to be the most important determinant of inter-industry performance differentials. Kumar (1985) used wages to sales ratio as a proxy to measure the quality of company's labour force. However, his results showed the associations of skill variable with growth as well as profitability to be negative and quite weak.

It is expected that the expenditure on employees would increase their satisfaction and efficiency as well. Hence, a positive linkage is expected between the expenditure on employees and financial performance of the firm. In line with Kumar (1985), skill variable has been computed by dividing the expenditure on salary and wages of employees and workers by sales. The qualifications and different categories of workers (viz. skilled, unskilled and semi-skilled) should have been taken into consideration, but the data were not available in the desired form. Hence this rather crude proxy has been used for skill variable.

Age

The age of a firm is an important determinant of performance. We expect that the older firms will outperform the younger ones. An old firm may grow faster and earn higher rate of return because it has established itself in the market and have certain core skills and experiences which its younger counterparts may not have. The profitable firms grow and survive, while inefficient/ unprofitable firms stagnate and exit the industry. Since the process takes time, larger firms are also older which in turn implies that there exists a positive age-profit relationship. Such a positive relationship can be reinforced by-learning-by-doing effect that makes firms more efficient as a result of their growing stock of experience. However, the converse can also be true if the older firms are not dynamic or flexible enough to keep pace with the changing technology (Chhibber and Majumdar, 1998; Sidhu and Bhatia, 1993).

Capital Intensity

Capital intensity has been measured in this study as the ratio of fixed assets to total sales. Firms are expected to shift from labour intensive methodology to capital intensive technology (by mechanising or modernising a process) with the anticipation that it would speed up the production process as well as improve the quality of product. It may also result in minimisation of wastage and reduction of cost of production and hence improved performance. As such, we set positive hypothesis with regard to capital intensity and performance on these lines.

However, capital intensity can also act as a barrier to exit. If a firm has invested a huge amount in fixed assets or for building plants, it may be compelled to remain in the same business even if it is declining because close down of business may result in huge loss (Porter, 1976). Moreover, if the cost of labour is lesser than the cost of capital, the firms with labour intensive technology may be more profitable than those which employ capital intensive technology (Sidhu and Bhatia, 1993).

Model

In order to sort out the effects of industry membership and firm characteristics on performance, the following models have been employed for the three different industry classification samples.

For Input Based Classification of Industries

$\rho = \beta_0 + \beta_1$ (Leverage) + β_2 (Capital Intensity) + β_3 (Risk) + β_4 (Age) + β_5 (Size) + β_6 (Skill) + β_7 (Metal Based Industry) + β_8 (Chemical Based Industry) + e.

For Use Based Classification of Industries

$\rho = \beta_0 + \beta_1$ (Leverage) + β_2 (Capital Intensity) + β_3 (Risk) + β_4 (Age) + β_5 (Size) + β_6 (Skill) + β_7 (Intermediate Goods Industry) + β_8 (Capital Goods Industry) + β_9 (Consumer Goods Industry) + e.

For Commodity/Activity-based Classification of Industries

$\rho = \beta_0 + \beta_1$ (Leverage) + β_2 (Capital Intensity) + β_3 (Risk) + β_4 (Age) + β_5 (Size) + β_6 (Skill) + β_7 (Automobile Industry) + β_8 (Cement Industry) + β_9 (Cotton Textile Industry) + β_{10} (Electrical Machinery Industry) + β_{11} (Fertiliser Industry) + β_{12} (Iron and

Steel Industry) + β_{13} (Jute Industry) + β_{14} (Man-made Fibre Industry) + β_{15} (Paint Industry) + β_{16} (Paper Industry) + β_{17} (Pharmaceutical Industry) + β_{18} (Sugar Industry) + β_{19} (Tea Industry) + β_{20} (Tobacco Industry) + β_{21} (Tyre and Tube Industry) + β_{22} (Vanaspati Industry) + β_{23} (Construction Industry) + β_{24} (Electricity Industry) + β_{25} (Shipping Industry) + β_{26} (Trading Industry) + e.

One industry dummy is omitted from each of the above three models to be served as the reference group (logic explained below).

Such models have been used by Hamilton and Shergill (1993) and Amato and Wilder (1990). We have computed these multiple regression models by using SPSS/PC$^+$ package on computer. Backward elimination method of stepwise ordinary least square regression has been used by specifying the criteria of removal of independent variables at 10 per cent level of significance. In the above models, firm specific variables are continuous variables while dummy variables have been used as independent variables to account for industry effects on performance. β_0 is the constant term, β_1, β_2, ... β_n are coefficients of independent variables while e indicates error term in our models.

Using binary (0,1) coding, dummy variables are always dichotomous variables. All firms which are member of a particular industry, are assigned a code of 1; firms not in that particular industry receive a code of 0. A categorical variable with *j* categories needs a set of *j*-1 dummy variables. The category not named as a dummy variable serves as the reference group. In our analysis, Aluminium industry, Basic goods industry and Agro-based Industry are the omitted dummy variables for respectively Commodity/Activity based, Use-based and Input-based industry classification samples. The rationales for including *j*-1 dummy variables in the regression models is that if all the binary variables were included, the normal regression equation will not be independent and so will not have a unique solution. For example, consider a model containing the dummy variable representing sex. 1 is coded for MALE respondent and 0 for the FEMALE respondent. If in addition to the dummy variable (MALE) coded 1, we include a second dummy variable (FEMALE) coded 0, it will be a model in which a perfect relationship exists between the two independent variables, because

$$\text{MALE} = 1 - \text{FEMALE}$$

Therefore, the information provided by FEMALE in the model is redundant and unnecessary to the estimation and it would provide a biased assessment of the impact of an independent variable.

β_0 in the above models includes, *inter alia*, the effect of 'excluded' industry category. The coefficients of the other industry variables represent the differential performance as compare to the excluded category. For example, in case of the model for Commodity/Activity-based industry classification, if β_0 is 0.20 and β_6 is 0.05, this would mean that firms in Automobile industry earn, on average, a 25 per cent return on the performance variable (GRTH or PRTF), which would be 5 points above the average for firms in Aluminium industry, the 'excluded' category in our model (For a detailed discussion on regression models with dummy variables see Hardy, 1993, pp. 75-97; Fox, 1984, pp. 73-85).

Regression models have to be used very carefully, otherwise they may produce very biased and misleading estimations. Various assumptions of OLS regression models have been tested to check that the regression assumptions as regarding the linearity and normal distribution of error term are met. Multicollinearity among independent variables may affect the overall estimations of the models as well as the coefficients of individual variables. We have computed VIF (Various Inflation Factor) on SPSS/PC$^+$ package on computer to determine the extent of collinearity among independent variables. The VIF is defined as under:

$$\text{VIF} = \frac{1}{(1 - R^2)}$$

where R is the multiple correlation coefficient when the ith independent variable is predicted from the other independent variables. The R^2 expresses the strength of linear relationship between the independent variables.

Non-linear Relations

The above models test only linear relationships. In other words they study the relationships between variables assuming the relationship between dependent and independent variables to be linear. However, even after meeting the assumptions underlying the application of straight line regression model, it does not guarantee that the model is appropriate. The scatter diagram of real-life data may reveal the presence of a non-linear relationship. Many non-linear models are available to study the non-linear relationships. But the statistical methods for handling non-linear relationships are more sophisticated and complicated in comparison to those which we use to study linear relationships. It is sometimes suggested to transform the data in order to linearize the relationship (Neter and Wasserman, 1974, Fox 1984). It has been tried to make the linear regression models more adequate by improving the linearity of variables through transformation. In this chapter, non-linear relationships have also been tried by transforming the control variables to logarithm, square and square root forms. Transformation of control variable has been done on the basis of its correlation with dependent variable. Only that form of transformation was selected which improved linearity the most.

Statistical Results

Tables 6.2 and 6.3 report the results of least squares estimations of regression equations which seek to decompose variation in performance in terms of industry effects and firm characteristics. These two Tables summarise the results of six regression models using GRTH and PRTF factors of performance respectively as dependent variables. Models 1, 2 and 3 are constructed respectively for the samples for Input-based, Use-based and Commodity/Activity-based industry classifications. Results have also been taken for three parallel models 1a, 2a and 3a, which contain explanatory variables of models 1, 2 and 3 respectively in transformed mode. The explanatory variables have been transformed in order to improve their linearity with dependent variables. We encountered no problems of outliers in all these regression models.

Table 6.2 contains regression results with GRTH as dependent variable. Risk and Skill variables are consistently significant in all the models at 1 per cent level, however, the former is positively and latter is negatively related to growth performance. Age has emerged as a hindrance to growth, but it has no significant impact in case of Commodity/Activity-based sample of industries. Capital intensity is influencing the growth of companies favourably, but it is not significant in case of Input-based sample as well as for model 2a of Use-based sample. Leverage is positively significant (at low level) in case of only model 3 which represents Commodity/Activity-based sample. Hence, leverage, capital intensity and age are not consistently significant in all the models.

Table 6.2 : Regression Coefficients (Standardised) for Firm and Industry Effects (Dependent Variable : GRTH)

Variable	Input Based Sample		Use Based Sample		Commodity/ Activity Based Sample	
	Model 1	Model 1a[1]	Model 2	Model 2a[1]	Model 3	Model 3a[2]
1	2	3	4	5	6	7
Constant Term	0.65 (3.42)*	1.91 (4.68)*	0.33 (1.63)	1.77 (5.28)*	-0.16 (-1.42)	-0.44 (-3.35)*
Leverage					0.13 (1.86)***	
Capital Intensity			0.14 (1.78)***		0.44 (6.21)*	0.45 (6.59)*
Risk	0.28 (3.12)*	0.26 (3.13)*	0.27 (3.57)*	0.26 (3.54)*	0.19 (2.94)*	0.22 (3.35)*
Age	-0.23 (-2.55)*	-0.28 (-3.33)*	-0.16 (-2.13)**	-0.24 (-3.37)*		
Skill	-0.23 (2.59)*	-0.32 (-3.71)*	-0.25 (-3.26)*	-0.31 (-4.61)*	-0.42 (-4.82)*	-0.45 (-5.25)*
Metal		0.19 (2.20)**				
Capital			0.17 (2.21)**	0.16 (2.23)*		

(Contd.)

Table 6.2 *(Contd.)*

1	2	3	4	5	6	7
Electrical Machinery					0.19 (2.60)*	0.18 (2.52)**
Sugar					0.12 (1.83)***	
Pharmaceutical					0.18 (2.56)**	0.16 (2.32)**
Cement					0.13 (1.84)***	
Tyre and Tube					0.21 (3.05)*	0.16 (2.36)**
Man-made Fibre					0.13 (1.94)***	
Paint					0.12 (1.81)***	0.13 (1.89)***
Automobile					0.23 (3.22)*	0.16 (2.52)**
Jute					0.20 (2.62)*	0.18 (2.28)**
Iron and Steel					0.13 (1.85)***	0.14 (1.90)***
Tea					0.17 (2.22)**	
Adjusted R^2	0.15	0.23	0.16	0.22	0.29	0.30
Number of Observations	110	110	152	152	171	171
F-Statistic	7.51* (3,106)	9.12* (4,105)	6.95* (5,146)	11.58* (4,147)	5.68* (15,155)	8.36* (10,160)

Notes: Figures in parentheses are t-ratios
* : Significant at 1 per cent level
** : Significant at 5 per cent level
*** : Significant at 10 per cent level
1. Age and Skill Variables in log form.
2. Capital Intensity Transformed to Square root form.
Models 1a, 2a and 3a have been constructed to contain explanatory variables of respectively models 1, 2 and 3 in transformed mode.

There are minor industry effects in respect of Input-based and Use-based samples but the same are important for Commodity/Activity-based sample of industries. Many industry groups of this classification are showing up favourable effects on the growth of the companies. F-Statistics are highly significant in all cases and the same have improved consistently for all the models containing variables in transformed mode. Adjusted R^2s have not explained a high variation in growth performance but they have improved slightly for the models with transformed data.

Table 6.3 shows regression results with PRTF as dependent

Table 6.3 : Regression Coefficients (Standardised) for Firm and Industry Effects (Dependent Variable : PRTF)

Variable	Input Based Sample		Use Based Sample		Commodity/ Activity Based Sample	
	Model 1	Model 1a[1]	Model 2	Model 2a[2]	Model 3	Model 3a[3]
Constant Term	1.15	4.81	0.96	1.78	0.69	1.76
	(5.56)*	(4.51)*	(6.17)*	(6.42)*	(5.40)*	(6.09)*
Leverage	-0.35	-0.37	-0.57	-0.5 8	-0.52	-0.54
	(-4.12)*	(4.45)*	(-8.63)*	(-8.93)*	(-9.43)*	(-11.40)*
Capital Intensity	-0.28	-0.52	-0.13	-0.16	-0.32	-0.44
	(-3.19)*	(-3.73)*	(-1.97)**	(-2.53)*	(-3.18)*	(-5.91)*
Risk		-0.15	-0.12	-0.14		
		(-1.89)***	(-1.75)***	(-2.14)**		
Age	-0.39	-0.41	-0.23	-0.30	-0.19	-0.25
	(-4.62)*	(-4.91)*	(-3.59)*	(-4.65)*	(-3.27)*	(-4.47)*
Intermediate			-0.17	-0.16		
			(-2.56)*	(-2.52)*		
Jute					-0.26	-0.26
					(-4.82)*	(-5.43)*
Tea					0.34	0.34
					(6.59)*	(6.92)*
Shipping					0.34	0.28
					(3.54)*	(4.15)*
Electricity					0.14	0.14
					(2.42)**	(2.70)*
Fertiliser					0.13	0.10
					(2.46)**	(2.15)**
Sugar						0.08
						(1.69)***
Trading						-0.08
						(-1.66)***
Adjusted R^2	0.28	0.34	0.39	0.42	0.55	0.63
Number of Observations	110	110	152	152	171	171
F-Statistic	14.90*	14.82*	20.11*	22.84*	27.20*	29.07*
	(3,106)	(4,105)	(5,146)	(5,146)	(8,162)	(10,160)

Notes: Figures in parentheses are t-ratios

* : Significant at 1 per cent level ** : Significant at 5 per cent level

*** : Significant at 10 per cent level.

1. Age, Risk and Leverage in Log term. 2. Age in log form

3. Leverage, Capital Intensity and Age transformed to square, square root and log form respectively.

Models 1a, 2a and 3a have been constructed to contain explanatory variables of respectively models 1, 2, and 3 in transformed mode.

variable. Leverage, Capital intensity and Age variables are related negatively and significantly with profitability all through. Risk is partially and negativity associated with PRTF and that too at lower level of significance. There are no significant industry effects in case of models 1 and 1a which represent samples for Input-based industry classification, while industry effects seem to be quite strong in case of models 3 and 3a constructed for Commodity/Activity-based industry classification. Only one industry, i.e. Intermediate goods segment is significantly different from the other in the analysis of Use-based sample. F-statistic is significant at 1 per cent level of significance in all the cases, which shows that all our models are adequate and appropriate. R^2 (adjusted coefficient of determinants) is maximum in case of models for Commodity/Activity-based industry classification, followed by models for Use-based sample. In all the three samples, by-models containing variables in transformed mode have improved R^2, and level of significance of certain variables' coefficients and have also picked some more variables. Except in case of Input-based sample, F-statistic also improved in all cases for the models with transformed data.

Discussion of Results

Industry effects are important mainly in respect of Commodity/Activity-based classification of industries, for both GRTH as well as PRTF. For Input-based classification, the positive impact of Metal-based industry on GRTH may be attributed to the Government which solved its problems and strengthened its competitive position. Similarly, for Use-based industry classification, the Capital goods industry may be favourable on GRTH because it has got special attention during the Sixth Plan (1980-85). Moreover, the budget for 1987-88 also announced certain incentives to this industry, e.g. technological upgradation. The Intermediate goods industry has shown a highly significant negative impact on profitability which might be due to the poor performance of some of its segments, viz. jute, man-made fibre and vanaspati industries on profitability front.

For Commodity/Activity-based model, electrical machinery, sugar, pharmaceutical, cement, tyre and tube, iron and steel, tea, man-made fibre, paint, automobile and jute industries are influencing the growth positively and significantly. Electrical machinery is a capital goods industry, which has been discussed just above. Sugar industry has become better mainly on account of the measures initiated by the Government, e.g. the ratio of free sale quota has been increased continuously over the period under our study. This industry has responded positively on the PRTF factor also. The investment and production in cement industry increased substantially after the partial decontrol of this industry since February 1982. The rapid growth of automobiles has increased the demand of tyre and tube industry to such an extent that the gap between domestic demand and supply has to be bridged through imports. This industry matches international standards in relation to technology and quality. The Government has provided various facilities to this industry also. Iron and steel industry is, by and large, in the hands of the State and as such it operates in a very controlled and protective environment. Moreover, the iron ore and coal required to this industry are available in close proximity. This industry is also self-sufficient technologically. Tea which is good on PRTF factor also, being a foreign exchange earning industry has been provided support by the Government in the form of loans and subsidies in order to boost its output. Man-made fibre industry has enjoyed a high time. It captured a big market share from the cotton textile by virtue of its distinctive qualities (discussed in detail in Chapter 5). Paint, an intermediate industry, performed well. The required raw material is available indigenously. Moreover, the import of finished paints has been restricted to a great extent. Pharmaceutical industry has also been a good performing industry. The Government has done certain favours to this industry like extension of delicensing from time to time (*Economic Survey* — various Issues). Due to ever increasing demand, automobile industry has done well on growth performance.

Electricity and fertiliser industries have good impact on PRTF. Electricity, or virtually the entire power sector is in the hands of the Government. Only nominal share of the total power generating capacity is in the hands of the private sector. This industry has no dearth of demand, however, the same sometimes suffers due to insufficient or late monsoon. Jute and shipping industries have shown up positively perhaps due to the omitted category (Aluminium) which is at the bottom in our analysis; and trading industry also seems to have shown up adverse impact on PRTF due to this reason. The Jute industry, however, has significant negative impact on profitability. Jute industry has been facing a number of problems, e.g. shortage of raw materials and power. Introduction of various substitute materials (like paper and cloth) has also hit this industry adversely.

Now we turn to the tentative reasons of why industry effects are strong only in models for Commodity/Activity-based industry classification. A comparison of the models 1, 1a, 2 and 2a with the models 3 and 3a suggests that the formers provide less explanatory power than the latters (R^2 are 0.28, 0.34, 0.39 and 0.42 respectively for the models 1, 1a, 2 and 2a while the same are 0.55 and 0.63 respectively for the models 3 and 3a). The models for Input-based and Use-based industry classifications include few number of industry categories grouped at more aggregate level. Conversely, the models for Commodity/Activity-based industry classification contain relatively much more number of industry groups categorised at more disaggregate level of industry products. Hence, it is apparent that the superiority of the models 3 and 3a comes from the level of aggregation for the industry variables pointing to the strength of the industry effects at the more disaggregate level of industry classification. This finding supports the view of Ahluwalia (1985) who suggests the analysis at a suitable level of disaggregation.

Our regression results have reported inverse relationship between profitability and capital intensity. The growth factor of performance, however, has positive relationship with capital intensity. The negative relationship between profitability and capital intensity is contrary to our hypothesis. As mentioned earlier, if two companies are having different degree of capital intensity but identical demand curves, marginal costs and average costs, the higher capital intensive company will have comparatively lower profitability. Moreover, if a firm has built up plant of excess capacity right from the beginning, the idle capacity may also cause low profitability resulting in negative relationship between capital intensity and profitability. Porter (1976) has stated that capital intensity can also act as a barrier to exit. If a firm has invested a huge amount in fixed assets or for building plant, it may be compelled to remain in the same business even if it is declining because close down of business may result in huge loss. Capital intensity, however, should be analysed separately for different industries as some industries by nature are technologically more capital intensive (e.g. Steel industry *versus* Tabacco/Tea industry).

Many researchers have revealed negative relationship between capital intensity and profitability. In capital intensive industries, sometimes producers part with profits in order to keep their plants operating at high activity levels. Sometimes, firms operating in growing capital intensive industries have to invest large amounts simply to keep pace with the industry (Pant 1991; also see Wagner, 1984). As regards the positive association of this variable with GRTH factor of performance, a highly capital intensive firm which has installed plant of large size and has strong infrastructure, may be in a position to tune up its activity at larger level.

There is strong negative relationship between risk and profitability consistently in three models. Our this finding is in line with those of Shepherd (1972), Armour and Teece (1978), Bowman (1980), Grant and Jammine (1988), Hamilton and Shergill (1993). Bowman attributed this to "good management". Good managers seek to achieve both higher profitability as well as low variation in earnings (Bowman, 1980, p. 25). Grant and Jammine on the other hand explained this outcome in terms of cost of capital. They asserted higher risk combined with leverage raised the cost of capital which in turn lowered profitability. In a study of New Zealand companies, Hamilton and Shergill (1993) contended that such relationship might be existing in New Zealand as a consequence of protection provided to some industries from internal and overseas competition which caused lower variation in earnings and higher profitability of companies (They measured risk as coefficient of variation in earnings per share). Shepherd (1972) measured risk by using the standard error of a trend line fitted to profit rates and reported a negative but insignificant association between risk and profit rates. He, however, stated this finding to be unexpected. Although Armour and Teece (1978) showed up a negative relationship between return on equity and variance of return on equity, it was not statistically significant. Risk and growth, however, are positively related which shows that these firms were extra cautious to manage their risky projects which led to the favourable performance in terms of growth of these firms. In other words, risk bearing is compensated by a higher rate of growth.

Leverage showed up to have adverse impact on profitability while the same has positive association with growth factor of performance. High leverage in our study denotes high proportion of debt capital employed in business in comparison to equity capital. The results of various studies witness diversity in respect of the relationship of leverage with performance and its measurement. Grant and Jammine (1988) reported high leverage to be associated with low profitability. Similarly, Chaganti and Damanpour (1991) revealed a negative correlation between long term debt to capital ratio and return on assets as well as return on equity. Equally, Arditti (1967) computed the ratio of debt to equity for leverage variable and found the sign of coefficient negative in his regressions. Leverage had also been found to be inversely related to the variability of earnings by Carleton and Silberman (1977). To the contrary, Baker (1973) measured leverage inversely by ratio of equity to assets and found that it had significantly negative sign in his simultaneous equation. In other words, larger amount of leverage (low value of leverage in his study) tended to raise profitability, where higher leverage reflected greater risks. In a study, Hall and Weiss (1967), along market structure variables, employed leverage, measured inversely as the ratio of equity to assets and found that it had a significantly positive effect on rate of return. Hamilton and Shergill (1993) revealed the impact of leverage (ratio of total debt to total assets) to be positive on return on equity, return on assets and growth of sales. However, they indicated that this relationship might vary over the business cycle.

The possible explanation of the negative relationship between leverage and profitability in the present study might be the interest expenses associated with heavy debt load. If a firm is highly levered and its rate of return on the company's assets is lower than the cost of debt capital, it will naturally lead to lower profitability. The association of high leverage with fast growth is also not unexpected. This finding is in line with Hamilton and Shergill (1993).

In an Indian study, Siddharthan and Dasgupta (1983) introduced, *inter alia*, skill variable in their profit equations. It turned out favourably the most important determinant of profitability. To the contrary, in our study, this variable has no significant association with profitability, while the same has a negative relationship with growth. One of the reasons for this discrepancy may be the difference with respect to measurement of this variable. Secondly, the underlying data have a great role to play (discussed subsequently in Chapter 8). The inverse relationship between skill and growth might be due to inefficiency of personnel, lack of co-operation and respond to changes in organisational structure. Further, use of ineffective or no personnel policy of the management might be the root cause of all these shortcomings.

Age has turned up to have negative relationship with both the factors of performance. The possible reasons for such relationship might be the persistent use of outdated management and marketing practices, obsolete technology by the old firms.

Summary and Conclusions

This chapter has sought to decompose the performance differentials in terms of industry effects and firm characteristic variables. For dependent variables, informations on six financial performance variables have been condensed through factor analysis into two composite factors, viz. GRTH and PRTF. Industry membership has turned up to be important particularly in respect of Commodity/Activity-based industry classification for both GRTH as well as PRTF. For the other two classification systems, contribution of industry is not consistently important for either of the performance indices. Capital intensity is related positively with growth and negatively with profitability. High capital intensity may provide infrastructure for growth but idle capacity may depress profitability as it adds to costs also. Risk has appeared with negative coefficeints in the models for PRTF. This might be the consequence of protection provided to some industries by the Government. Inversely, it can also be attributed to good management skill which endeavour to maximise profitability with minimum variations in rate of return. Risk and growth, however, are positively related which shows that the firms were extra cautious to manage their risky projects which led to the favourable performance in terms of growth of these firms. In other words, risk bearing is compensated by a higher rate of growth.

Exactly, like capital intensity, leverage too has negative association with profitability and positive association with growth. The linkage of high leverage with fast growth is not unexpected. Firms can find it handy to depend on borrowed capital for the expansion of business in order to cash some opportunity. But the heavy interest expenses, the corollary of heavy debt load may lower rate of profit. Skill, measured as the ratio of wages and salaries to sales, is negatively related to growth. The higher expenditure on workers and employees might not be fruitful due to the use of faulty or ineffective personnel policy by the management. Age has inverse association both with profitability as well as growth, probably due to all the weaknesses which an oldman can have.

7

MARKET STRUCTURE AND PERFORMANCE

Introduction

The field of industrial organisation assumes the market structure variables to be the determinants of performance. The main elements of market structure are market share, concentration and barriers to entry. Bain's study (1951) is the pioneering work in this field. His work was followed by a number of researchers investigating the relationship between market structure and economic performance in industrially advanced countries. Many policies have been framed on the basis of the findings of such studies specially with regard to monopolies. However, there has been virtually negligible number of studies on this subject in less developed countries (LDCs). Except two or three industry based studies, there is as yet no comprehensive firm level study in India on this subject. This chapter has sought to fill this gap. The theoretical framework underlying market structure-performance relationship is detailed in Chapter 4. Linear regression models have been employed to decompose industry effects and to discover the contribution of some variables representing firm and market characteristics in explaining performance differentials among industries.

Sample

The sample to be analysed in this chapter is different from the one used in Chapter 6. Number of companies as well as number of industries have to be truncated on account of non-availability of data on certain additional variables to be investigated in this chapter for all the original companies and industries. For this

Table 7.1 : Make up of Sample for Market Structure-Performance Analysis

Industry Group		Number of Companies
Commodity Based Classification		
1.	Aluminium	04
2.	Automobile	10
3.	Cement	10
4.	Cotton Textile	08
5.	Fertilisers	06
6.	Iron and Steel	09
7.	Jute	07
8.	Man-made Fibre	13
9.	Paint	06
10.	Paper	10
11.	Sugar	09
12.	Tea	10
13.	Tobacco	04
14.	Tyre and Tube	09
15.	Vanaspati	04
	Total	119
Use Based Classification		
1.	Basic Goods	29
2.	Intermediate Goods	39
3.	Capital Goods	07
4.	Consumer Goods	48
	Total	123
Input Based Classification		
1.	Agro Based	51
2.	Metal Based	14
3.	Chemical Based	25
	Total	90

chapter, Commodity-based industry classification sample contains 119 companies spread over 15 industries. The Use-based industry classification consists of 123 companies divided in four industry groups and there are 90 companies in Input-based industry classification grouped into three industry categories. Table 7.1

below provides the detailed break up of samples for three different industry classifications.

Performance

Performance has been measured on the same lines as was done in Chapters 5 and 6. Performance has been defined along two dimensions, namely profitability and growth.* ROE (Return on Equity) and ROA (Return on Assets) have been chosen as the indicators of profitability, while GSALES (Growth in Sales), GTNA (Growth in Total Net Assets) and GDIV (Growth in Dividends) have been taken to represent growth. The composite index of performance has been constructed through factor analysis. The procedure of which is explained in detail in Chapter 5. Here we shall give it only a brief touch. The results of factor analysis are set out in Tables 7.2 to 7.10 below separately for the three different industry classifications.

Table 7.2 : Factor Structure and Commonalities of Performance Variables : Input-based Classification

Variable	Commonalities	Factor	Eigen Value	% of Variance	Cumulative
ROE	0.74536	1	2.42825	48.6	48.6
ROA	0.78753	2	1.25382	25.1	73.7
GSALES	0.88083				
GTNA	0.78022				
GDIV	0.48814				

Trace = 5.0

Table 7.3 : Varimax (Orthogonal) Factor Matrix of Performance Variables : Input Based Classification

Variable	Factor I	Factor II
ROE	0.26022	0.82319
ROA	0.00961	0.88738
GSALES	0.93760	0.04170
GTNA	0.87652	0.10922
GDIV	0.66994	0.19831

* The choice of performance indicaters has been discussed in details in Chapter 3.

Table 7.4 : Factor Score Coefficient Matrix of Performance Variables : Input Based Classification

Variable	Factor	
	I-GRTH	II-PRTF
ROE	−0.00285	0.54318
ROA	−0.13815	0.62917
GSALES	0.46078	−0.12139
GTNA	0.41945	−0.06356
GDIV	0.30209	0.03304

Table 7.5 : Factor Structure and Commonalities of Performance Variables : Use Based Classification

Variable	Commonalities	Factor	Eigen Value	% of Variance	Cumulative
ROE	0.69205	1	2.32992	46.6	46.6
ROA	0.73243	2	1.17503	23.5	70.1
GSALES	0.83803				
GTNA	0.78602				
GDIV	0.45642				

Trace = 5.0

Table 7.6: Varimax Rotated (Orthogonal) Factor Matrix of Performance Variables : Use Based Classification

Variable	Factor I	Factor II
ROE	0.21505	0.80362
ROA	0.04566	0.85460
GSALES	0.91539	0.01003
GTNA	0.87730	0.12791
GDIV	0.61777	0.27345

Table 7.7 : Factor Score Co-efficient Matrix of Performance Variables : Use-based Classification

Variable	Factor	
	I-GRTH	II-PRTF
ROE	−0.03214	0.55865
ROA	−0.13228	0.62767
GSALES	0.48880	−0.16044
GTNA	0.44676	−0.06572
GDIV	0.28096	−0.09020

Table 7.8 : Factor Structure and Commonalities of Performance Variables : Commodity-based Classification

Variable	Commonalities	Factor	Eigen Value	% of Variance	Cumulative
ROE	0.69364	1	2.33260	46.7	46.7
ROA	0.73305	2	1.17848	23.6	70.3
GSALES	0.83820				
GTNA	0.78714				
GDIV	0.45906				

Trace = 5.0

Table 7.9 : Varimax Rotated (Orthogonal) Factor Matrix of Performance Variables : Commodity-based Classification

Variable	Factor I	Factor II
ROE	0.21474	0.80469
ROA	0.04456	0.85502
GSALES	0.91547	0.01034
GTNA	0.87835	0.12503
GDIV	0.61678	0.28042

Table 7.10 : Factor Score Coefficient Matrix of Performance Variables : Commodity-based Classification

Variable	Factor	
	I-GRTH	II-PRTF
ROE	−0.03222	0.55731
ROA	−0.13262	0.62578
GSALES	0.48865	−0.15990
GTNA	0.44777	−0.06807
GDIV	0.27917	0.09502

Exactly like the outcome of the analysis in Chapter 5, the factor analysis technique here also has extracted two factors for each of the three industry classifications adopted for this study. Tables 7.4, 7.7 and 7.10 contain the compositions of these factors for the three classifications. We again named them as growth (GRTH) and profitability (PRTF). In all the three cases, more than 70 per cent of the total variance is explained by these two factors (see Tables 7.2, 7.5 and 7.8) which is well above the acceptable limit, i.e. 60 per cent (Bourgeois 1985).* The composite performance indices for our three different industry classification samples are obtained by further processing the factor score coefficients by employing the same methodology which we adopted in Chapter 5.

Hypotheses and Variables

Apart from the variables used in Chapter 5, certain additional variables have been added in this chapter to examine the relationship between market structure and performance. These are—market share, concentration ratio and capacity utilisation. In this section only these three variables will be discussed as other variables have been dealt with in detail in Chapter 6.

* However, Zaltman and Burger (1975) suggested the acceptable limit to be greater than 40 per cent.

Market Share

Market Share shows the extent of a firm's control over the market and indicates its position in the market. A positive relationship has been reported between market share and rate of return in a number of empirical studies (Gale, 1972; Shepherd, 1972, 1979; Catry and Chavalie, 1974; Ravenscraft, 1983; Wagner, 1984). Market share is defined as the sales of the company divided by the sales of the industry. We multiplied this ratio by 100 to depict market share in percentage. The association between market share and performance is expected to be positive for the following reasons:

(a) Companies with large market share may have products of higher quality which enable them to charge higher prices than their small counterparts;
(b) Companies with large market share may be more efficient on account of scale economies;
(c) Companies with larger shares may be more innovative (Ravenscraft, 1983; Gale, 1972).

However, the relationship between market share and performance may be curvi-linear because of inefficiency at high shares. This relationship may also prove to be negative on account of 'Umbrella Pricing' (Shepherd, 1972). Data on market share have been collected from CMIE's publications 'Markets and Market Shares'. However, in case, a company is producing more than one type of commodity, we have worked out the weighted average of the same. We have averaged the market shares of different years within our study period to get the average rate for our analysis. The computation procedure is detailed subsequently in this section.

Seller Concentration

Theoretical framework and measurement of seller concentration have been discussed at length in Chapter 4. At one time, industry concentration was considered the only element of market structure (see, Bain, 1951). Industrial concentration refers to the extent of a particular market in the hands of a few firms. It describes the state of competitive condition prevalent in the market of a particular product which may range from perfect competition to pure monopoly. Oligopoly theory suggests that manipulation of price and output of a product depend on the number and size distribution of firms in a particular market. A high seller concentration would mean market power (control over price and output) in the hands of a few large firms and in such cases there is greater probability of successful collusion among these firms. The collusion may be implicit or tacit. A perfect collusion would enable the sellers to manipulate price and output behaviour in such a way as to produce monopoly profits. Hence, seller concentration is likely to be positively related to financial performance (Bain, 1951; Chamberlin, 1962; Stigler, 1964). However, there is an other school of thoughts which asserts that a positive concentration-performance relationship may not always be on account of collusive or monopolistic practices among the few large firms having control over the market. This relationship may be positive due to the efficiency and/or scale economies of large firms (Demsetz, 1973).

Concentration in this study is measured by the share of industry sales accounted for by the four largest companies in the industry. This is the most widely used measure of concentration. The data on the shares of the four largest firms have been compiled from the CMIE's publication 'Markets and Market Shares'. However, this information was available for only the five years of our 11 years study period. We constructed four-firm concentration ratio for five years by compiling the data from the so-called CMIE's publication 'Markets and Market Shares' of the years June 1983, March 1986, November 1989, February 1991 and March 1992 which provided information respectively for the years 1980-81, 1983-84, 1987-88, 1989-90 and 1990-91. An average of the degree of concentration of these five years was taken to be used in multivariate models. This industry characterising variable has been sought to be employed at the maximum possible disaggregate level of the industry products.

Put differently, concentration ratios have been constructed in such a way that each company is assigned the concentration ratio of only that product group in which it competes. For instance, in automobile industry, companies producing heavy commercial vehicles and two wheelers have been assigned concentration ratios of their respective two products groups.

Capacity Utilisation

Optimum utilisation of existing capacity reduces the cost of production and also accelerates growth. As exports play an important role in the economy of developing countries (as they depend very much on other countries), optimum utilisation of capacity enables such countries to increase their output economically which, in turn, augments their exports and also helps them in import substitution (for empirical research and references on this subject see Kaur, 1992).

Many researchers have analysed the impact of capacity utilisation on profitability. In one of the earliest works on capacity utilisation, Harrod (1933-34) reported that in imperfect competition if the layouts operated below the optimum capacity, its profits were also below the optimum level. Ramappa (1970) interpreted the low industrial productivity and profitability during 1966 to 1968 to be the consequence of idle industrial capacity during this period. Gupta and Thavaraj (1975) in an Indian study used a sample of fertiliser units to investigate the relationship between cost, profitability and capacity utilisation. They found that underutilisation of capacity increased cost of production which, in turn, decreased profits. In an analysis of the extent of idle capacity in sugar industry, Pittie (1975) found that Rs. 235 crores could have been saved and the production of sugar could have been increased by six lakh tons if the whole idle capacity had been utilised during the normal tenure of six months for the crushing season. In the analysis of capacity utilisation and profitability of Durgapur Steel Plant over the years 1964-65 to 1971-72, Mishra (1977) found that lowering of capacity utilisation was not followed by proportionate reduction in costs. As fixed costs were a significant proportion of the total costs, higher utilisation helped in boosting the profitability. On the basis of the study of six firms in bicycle industry of Ludhiana, Bajaj (1977-78) had also supported the existence of high degree of positive correlation between excess capacity and average variable cost. Satyanarayan and Sarma (1979) came across the similar results on the basis of investigation of Indian Public Sector for the year 1968-69. On the basis of theoretical grounds and prior research, a positive relationship is expected between capacity utilisation and profitability. The higher level of capacity utilisation would reduce the cost of production especially because the fixed costs do not increase proportionately with the increase in capacity utilisation and production (Amjad, 1977).

There are number of methods to measure capacity and capacity utilisation, e.g. Peak-Output method, Production-Function method, Time-Intensity method. We have used Peak-Output method to measure capacity utilisation rate in our study. This is a simple and widely used method to measure capacity-utilisation. Moreover, in the light of availability of data and nature of our sample, only this method suits us the most. Our sample contains companies from various industries of different natures. In some industries, companies have over-built their capacities in view of the future growth and expansion of demand, availability of inputs and skilled labour etc. However, even the company with the highest production in certain industries has used even a small fraction of its installed capacity, e.g. companies in sugar industry. Dhampur Sugar Mills Ltd. company had the maximum production of 157.40 thousand tonnes among all the companies in sugar industry for the year ending March 1991, whereas it had installed capacity of 4,000 thousand tonnes.

The Peak-Output method compares company's actual output during the year with the maximum output attained by that company in that industry. In terms of formula it can be expressed as under:

$$\text{Capacity Utilisation Rate} = \frac{\text{Production of the company within the year}}{\text{Maximum production attained by that company in that industry}} \times 100$$

In case of multi-product companies, weighted average method has been used to compute capacity utilisation and market share, taking sales revenue of respective products as weights. The data for computing capacity utilisation rate have been collected from CMIE's publication 'Markets and Market Shares'.

Model

This chapter aims to test how market structure may affect performance. We have employed model consisting determinants of both structure and profits. The main determinants of structure are market share, concentration and barriers to entry. Such models have been employed widely by the researchers to study the market structure-profitability relationships, e.g. by Bain 1951, 1956, Shepherd 1972, 1979, Amato and Wilder, 1990. The relationships have been assumed to be linear. However, to improve the linearity, some variables have been transformed to logarithm, square and square root form, and the results have been taken separately by employing transformed data in the model. Transformation of control variables has been done on the basis of correlation of control variables with dependent variables. Only that mode of transformation was selected which improved linearity the most.

There may be interaction effects among the independent variables, which affect overall estimations of the model as well as the coefficients of individual variables. We have employed a statistical test called VIF* (Variance Inflation Factor) to determine the strength of the interaction effects among the independent variables. The models for testing market structure's effects on performance for the three different industry classifications are given as under:

---

* The Variance Inflation Factor (VIF), which is defined as $1/1-r^2$, shows how variance of an estimator is inflated by the presence of multicollinearity. As a rule of thumb, if the VIF of a variable exceeds 10 that variable is said to be highly collinear (Kleinbaum, Kupper, and Mueller, 1988, Gujrati, 1995).

For Input Based Classification of Industries

$\rho = \beta_0 + \beta_1$ (Leverage) + β_2 (Capital Intensity) + β_3 (Risk) + β_4 (Age) + β_5 (Size) + β_6 (Skill) + β_7 (Capacity Utilisation) + β_8 (Market Share) + β_9 (Concentration Ratio) + β_{10} (Metal Based Ind.) + β_{11} (Chemical Based Ind.) + e

For Use Based Classification of Industries

$\rho = \beta_0 + \beta_1$ (Leverage) + β_2 (Capital Intensity) + β_3 (Risk) + β_4 (Age) + β_5 (Size) + β_6 (Skill) + β_7 (Capacity Utilisation) + β_8 (Market Share) + β_9 (Concentration Ratio) + β_{10} (Intermediate Goods Ind.) + β_{11} (Capital Goods Ind.) + β_{12} (Consumer Goods Ind.) + e

For Commodity Based Classification of Industries

$\rho = \beta_0 + \beta_1$ (Leverage) + β_2 (Capital Intensity)+ β_3 (Risk) + β_4 (Age) + β_5 (Size) + β_6 (Skill) + β_7 (Capacity Utilisation) + β_8 (Market Share) + β_9 (Concentration Ratio) + β_{10} (Automobile Ind.) + β_{11} (Cement Ind.) + β_{12} (Cotton Textile Ind.) + β_{13} (Fertiliser Ind.) + β_{14} (Iron & Steel Ind.) + β_{15} (Jute Ind.) + β_{16} (Man-made Fibre Ind.) + β_{17} (Paint Ind.) + β_{18} (Paper Ind.) + β_{19} (Sugar Ind.) + β_{20} (Tea Ind.) + β_{21} (Tobacco Ind.) + β_{22} (Tyre and Tube Ind.) + β_{23} (Vanaspati Ind.) + e

One industry dummy is excluded from each of the above three models to be served as the reference group (logic explained in Chapter 6).

We are very much interested to know whether the effects of independent variables are the same for all industry groups, or whether industry group differences also exist. We have constructed a set of dummy variables to capture the information contained in industry categorisation and then used this information in a multiple regression estimations. These multiple regression equations have been solved on computer by using SPSS/PC$^+$ package. Backward elimination producer of stepwise OLS regression has been employed by setting the removal criteria at 10 per cent level of significance. β_0 is the intercept, β_1, β_2, β_3......β_n are the coefficients of independent variables and *e* depicts the error term in the above models. All variables in the above models are continuous variables except industry categories which are dummy variables. The dummy variables are explained in detailed in Chapter 6.

Statistical Results

The results of the regression equations which we run for different industry classification samples, are condensed in Tables 7.11 and 7.12 separately for respectively Growth and Profitability as the dependent variables. We have tested two regression equations for each sample. In the first models, independent variables have been employed in their simple form of computation, while in the second models of each industry classification sample, we have sought to improve linearity by transforming the variables into log, square or squareroot form.

Table 7.11 reports the determinants of growth performance. The independent variables which are common in the regression analysis of Chapters 6 and 7, show almost similar trend. Risk has turned out to be a favourable factor for growth performance and is significant in all the equations. Age and skill have negative impacts on growth, but both are insignificant for Commodity-based sample. Leverage and capital intensity have eased growth significantly in case of only Commodity-based sample. Size has shown a strong inverse relationship with growth for Commodity-based sample only. Concentration has negative influence on growth in only transformed model for Input-based sample, but it has very low significance level (10%). The coefficient of market share is positive but significant at very low level in model 1 for Input-based sample. The same is strongly positive in model 3 for Commodity-based sample, however the level of significance has dropped considerably in non-linear model of this classification. Some of the industry segments are important to growth in all our samples. F-statistic is significant at 1-per cent level of significance. Moreover, the same has improved considerably for the models with transformed data of all the samples.

Table 7.11 : Regression Coefficients (Standardised) for Market Structure and Performance (Dependent Variable : GRTH)

Variable	Input Based Sample		Use Based Sample		Commodity/ Based Sample	
	Model 1	Model 1a[1]	Model 2	Model 2a[2]	Model 3	Model 3a[3]
Constant Term	0.57	2.34	0.25	1.61	1.97	0.84
	(2.60)*	(4.32)*	(1.64)*	(4.17)*	(2.70)*	(1.22)
Leverage					0.23	0.26
					(2.56)**	(2.97)*
Capital Intensity					0.22	0.18
					(2.35)**	(2.05)**
Risk	0.26	0.24	0.24	0.24	0.18	0.14
	(2.63)*	(2.61)**	(2.88)*	(3.02)*	(2.03)**	(1.73)***
Age	-0.21	-0.32	-0.23	-0.27		
	(-2.08)**	(-3.50)*	(-2.68)*	(-3.36)*		
Skill	-0.20	-0.35		-0.22		
	(-2.01)**	(-3.35)*		(-2.66)*		
Size					-0.35	-0.25
					(-3.15)*	(-0.71)*
Market Share	0.22				0.29	0.18
	(1.82)***				(2.65)*	(1.95)***
Concentration		-0.22				
		(-1.79)***				
Metal	0.32	0.35				
	(2.70)*	(3.07)*				
Capital			0.22	0.22		
			(2.65)*	(2.79)*		
Tobacco					0.21	0.21
					(2.45)**	(2.52)**
Paper					0.15	
					(1.73)***	
Tyre & Tube					0.39	0.35
					(4.48)*	(4.08)*
Cotton Textile					0.16	
					(1.78)***	
Fertilisers					0.17	
					(1.94)***	
Tea					-0.24	-0.17
					(-2.60)*	(-2.31)**
Adjusted R^2	0.19	0.26	0.14	0.22	0.21	0.20
Number of Observations	90	90	123	123	119	119
F - Statistics	5.07*	7.39*	7.81*	9.50*	3.83*	5.09*
	(5,84)	(5,84)	(3,119)	(4,118)	(10,108)	(7,111)

Notes: Figures in parenthesis are t-ratios

* : Significant at 1 per cent level. ** : Significant at 5 per cent level.

*** : Significant at 10 per cent level.

1. Age and skill in log form. 2. Age and Skill in log form.

3. Risk, Capital Intensity and Market Share in Square form; Leverage and Size in log form.

Models 1a, 2a and 3a have been constructed to contain explanatory variables of models 1, 2 and 3 respectively in transformed mode.

The adjusted R^2, however, has decreased slightly for such model of Commodity-based classification of industry.

Exactly like the results in Chapter 6, leverage, capital intensity and age are consistently negative and significant in all the models regressed on profitability. Risk also has negative coefficient, however, it is significant at low level in equations for Input-based industry classification and it is not significant for model 3 of Commodity-based sample. Unlike in Chapter 6, size has emerged significant at 5 per cent level in some equations with positive coefficient. Regarding the relationships of additional variables introduced in this chapter with profitability, there is no consistency in terms of significance. The capacity utilisation is positively significant solely in model 1a, where it has been employed in square form. Market share is also positive and significant in absolute as well as in square form but only in the models for Commodity-based samples. Concentration has negative and significant association with profitability in all our equations except for the equations for Use-based industry sample. The concentration has been employed in square mode in model 1a of Input-based sample and in log form of transformation in model 3a representing sample for Commodity-based industry classification.

Coming to the importance of industry groups in different industry classifications, profitability is not sensitive to any industry segment of Input-based industry sample, while only one industry category is showing superiority of profitability in Use-based classification. In model 3 for Commodity-based sample, four industry categories are showing significant impact on profitability and only two of them are strong for model 3a which employs continuous variables in transformed mode. The F-statistic is highly significant in all equations. Moreover, F-statistic as well as adjusted R^2 has improved in all our models with transformed data. This suggests that the models which employ variables in transformed mode, are more appropriate and more adequate. We checked multicollinearity in the models by examining the variance inflation factors (VIF) for each independent variable. Although

Table 7.12: Regression Coefficients (Standardised) for Market Structure and Performance (Dependent Variable : PRTF)

Variable	Input Based Sample		Use Based Sample		Commodity/ Based Sample	
	Model 1	Model 1a[1]	Model 2	Model 2a[2]	Model 3	Model 3a[3]
Constant Term	-0.95	2.20	1.02	5.23	1.17	5.62
	(-0.76)	(1.37)	(5.51)*	(6.17)*	(5.60)*	(7.16)*
Leverage	-0.41	-0.39	-0.59	-0.64	-0.52	-0.59
	(-4.53)*	(-4.78)*	(-8.54)*	(-9.95)*	(-9.14)*	(-10.74)*
Capital Intensity	-0.35	-0.41	-0.19	-0.29	-0.23	-0.27
	(-3.77)*	(-4.57)*	(-2.90)*	(-4.44)*	(-4.16)*	(-4.95)*
Risk	-0.15	-0.16	-0.13	-0.25		-0.25
	(-1.70)***	(-2.04)**	(-1.95)*	(-3.98)*		(-4.63)*
Age	-0.50	-0.55	-0.38	-0.46	-0.26	-0.33
	(-5.66)*	(-6.72)*	(-5.59)*	(-7.23)*	(-4.13)*	(-5.60)*
Size	0.22	0.25		0.14		
	(2.10)**	(2.41)**		(2.28)**		
Capacity Utilisation		0.24				
		(2.70)*				
Market Share					0.21	0.12
					(2.63)*	(2.16)**
Concentration	-0.26	-0.25			-0.65	-0.14
	(-2.42)**	(-2.66)*			(-3.07)*	(-2.52)*
Consumer			0.20	0.18		
			(2.95)*	(2.96)*		
Tyre & Tube					0.10	
					(1.75)***	
Jute					-0.24	-0.26
					(-4.10)*	(-4.96)*
Tea					0.37	0.29
					(6.52)*	(5.25)*
Fertiliser					0.18	
					(3.17)*	
Adjusted R^2	0.38	0.49	0.48	0.57	0.65	0.70
Number of Observations	90	90	123	123	119	119
F- Statistics	10.17*	13.19*	23.29*	27.66*	25.87*	35.27*
	(6,83)	(7,82)	(5,117)	(6,116)	(9,109)	(8,110)

Notes: Figures in parentheses are t-ratios.
* : Significant at 1 per cent level.
** : Significant at 5 per cent level.
*** : Significant at 10 per cent level.
1. Capacity utilisation and concentration ratio in square form; Age, risk, leverage and size in log form.
2. Age and Risk in log form; Size in square root form.
3. Risk, Age and Concentration ratio in log form; Market Share in square form.
Models 1a, 2a and 3a have been constructed to contain explanatory variables of respectively models 1, 2 and 3 in transformed mode.

size, capacity utilisation, market share and concentration are highly correlated with one another, they did not create any problem of multicollinearity. The VIFs for each of these variables in all our models ranged from 1.11 to 2.23 which is well below the upper limit of 10, suggesting that multicollinearity is not a concern (Neter *et al.*, 1989).

Although a number of continuous variables as well as industry dummy variables are common to the analysis of Chapter 6 and 7, yet certain changes are seen as regards the behaviours of these so-called common variables. For example, size is not significant at all in the analysis in Chapter 6, but the same is significant in this chapter for both growth and profitability performance though partially, i.e. not for all the equations. Similarly there exists noticeable changes in connection with industry segments. This all directly suggests that results are sensitive to number of variables in the equation and number of observation in the sample. This may also be taken to explain as to why the results of different researchers differ though they use the same models.

Discussion of Results

The main attraction of this chapter is the findings relating to market-share/concentration-performance relationship. Before discussing the findings on this association we would summarise as to how such findings are generally interpreted.

There are two schools of thought in industrial economics, which interpret concentration-profitability relationship differently, namely—traditional and revisionist. Based on the empirical relationship between profit rates and market concentration, the traditional view posits that high concentration leads to collusion, poor performance and higher profits. The revisionists, however, suggest that the observed empirical relationship between profitability and concentration results from firm level efficiencies that elevate both the market share and profits of large firms. In brief, the traditional view lay emphasis on collusion, while the revisionist view emphasises on the efficiency of the firms in explaining the profit-concentration relationship.

In the recent past, many researchers in the field of industrial economics have attempted to test the revisionist and traditional views of the structure-performance relationship. They have related the cross-sectional variations in rate of return to market share by treating it as a proxy for efficiency, and market concentration by taking it as a proxy for collusive opportunities. Many of them (viz. Shepherd, 1972; Branch, 1980; Gale and Branch, 1982; Ravenscraft, 1983; Amato and Wilder, 1990) suggest that the profitability is more strongly related to market share than to concentration. The revisionists take this finding to prove that efficiency is more important than collusion in explaining cross-sectional dispersion in rate of return. However, Shepherd (1972) has interpreted his finding of the positive relationship between market share and rate of return in a different way. Unlike revisionists, he has ascribed the importance of market share to market power rather than to efficiency.

Further, the proxies taken for efficiency and collusion are very crude. As adequate proxies are not possible owing to insufficiency of detailed data, an alternative empirical approach has been put forth by Schmalensee (1985) to capture firm and industry effects which uses, *inter alia* market share, concentration and industry dummy variables. The approach suggested by Schemalensee has also been used by Scott and Pascoe (1986), Amato and Wilder (1990) and Hamilton and Shergill (1993). We, too, have applied the same in our study.

Hypothesis of a positive influence of market share on performance is supported mainly for Commodity-based sample (see Tables 7.11 and 7.12). High market share is often supposed to offer some advantages to the businesses such as economies of scale, brand-name dominance, and greater bargaining power with suppliers, distributors and customers. Consequently businesses that have high market shares are usually more profitable than those with a low share. Schwalbach (1991) states that companies with high market share are rewarded by higher returns because they are in a position to satisfy customers' needs better than their smaller counterparts. Phillips (1976) on the other hand concludes that high profits may cause market concentration or conversely, market concentration and high profits may be the result of superior performance. To Catry and Chevalie (1974), high market share may lead to high profits on account of the concept of break-even: the higher the sales, the higher the profit. Ravenscraft (1983) put forth three possibilities underlying the positive association between market share and profits. First, companies with large market shares may be producing high quality products enabling them to sell their products at higher prices than the companies with small shares. Second, companies with larger shares may be more efficient due to scale economies. Finally, companies with large shares may be more innovative and creative. Apart from scale economies, management quality or simply luck may also contribute to the positive link between market share and profitability. Moreover, large share may represent concentration which may induce collusive behaviour and higher prices.

Jacobson and Aeker (1985), however, did not find the direct impact of market share on ROI as strong as had widely been assumed. They believed that apart from the emphasis on the attainment of high market share, the firms should give equal or greater importance to other key areas also such as product quality, customer satisfaction, productivity, corporate culture, product line appropriateness and management effectiveness. It should, nevertheless, be kept in mind that though high market share generally yields high profitability; gaining market share have adverse effect as it often entails huge investments. Negative results have also been reported relating to market share (see, Amato and Wilder, 1990; Porter, 1979).

Our results do not support the hypothesis that the four-firm concentration variable is a proxy for the ability to collude. Contrary to the traditional relationship, our study has revealed a significantly negative relationship between concentration and profitability in both the models of Input-based and Commodity-based samples. Although in one of the six equations the relationship between concentration and growth is negative, yet it is statistically weak (significant only at 10% level). In other words our study indicates that high concentration would lower profitability. It suggests that in Indian industries, high concentration or monopoly ushers inefficiency and poor performance which, in turn, depress profitability. The positive but weak relationship revealed by some Indian studies may be due to inadequacy of model specifications. For example, none of them has employed market share in their models. With the absence of this variable in the model, concentration may reflect the impact of market share on profitability.

Gale reported in the footnote of his 1972 paper that in multivariate regression equation respective signs of coefficients of market share and concentration were positive and negative and the former was comparatively more important. Gale and Branch (1982) discovered that when market share and concentration were both included in a model explaining profitability, the importance of concentration was insignificant. In similar vein, Ravenscraft (1983) also found that profits declined with concentration when other variables such as market share were held constant. Significantly, when he omitted the market share variable in the industry equation, concentration changed from significantly negative to significantly positive. In the study of Chappell and Cottle (1985) also, concentration turned insignificant when efficiency variables were included as determinants of profitability. The concentration coefficient was even negative in three of the four regressions. The results of Cubbin and Geroski (1987) also showed the coefficient of concentration to be negative when employed with market share variable. Holtermann's (1973) results also lend no support to the hypothesis that firms in highly concentrated industries earn super normal profits. The possible explanation for this finding in his own opinion is that X-inefficiency arises from the inefficient use of capital and it outweighs the effect on profits of excess prices charged in the monopolistic industries. This shows up in a low rate of return on assets (ROA). Hence our finding of negative relationship between concentration and profitability is not surprising. This is consistent with some previous works involving firm data.

Capacity utilisation has shown up positive and highly significant in relation to profitability in only one model of Input-based industry sample. This finding is in line with the widely reported results. This association might be due to the fact that increased utilisation of installed capacity would have resulted in the reduction of per unit fixed costs. Fixed costs generally remain constant for the level of installed capacity and the increase of operation upto this level will result in reduction of per unit as well as overall cost of production. Apart from this, economies of finance, purchasing and marketing can also be derived by operating at larger level. Furthermore, idle capacity represents the block of capital without any return thereon. The results relating to leverage, capital intensity, risk, age and skill variables are identical with the ones in Chapter 6 and they have been discussed there. The size variable, however, has turned significant in this chapter for both GRTH as well as PRTF. There is a significant positive relationship between size and PRTF which reflect scale economies and market power (Montgomery, 1979; Hamilton and Shergill, 1993). Apart from scale economies, a large firm may earn higher returns on account of technical factors (like specialisation and division of labour, better organisation), marketing factors (like cheap availability of raw material and efficient selling of products), financial factors (like ability to raise working capital easily from banks) (Kaur, 1997). A larger firm may be earning higher returns because it has all the options which a smaller firm has, and in addition it can take up the projects requiring heavy investment. Hall and Weiss (1967) also ascribed the positive relationship of size with profitability to easy access to capital markets and technical efficiencies due to increased capital intensity. A negative relationship has also been found by some researchers. Marcus (1969) found that the association between firm size and profitability within industries was not systematic. Some industries exhibited positive relations, some negative and others no relations at all. Shepherd (1972) also found the size to be negatively associated with profitability in all cases at high confidence level. He stated that the negative coefficient seemed to be caused by X-inefficiency, because the size raises not only market power but costs also.

Although it is widely accepted that big firms enjoy economies of large scale which, in turn, results in higher returns, yet our regression results do not reveal any such superiority of big firms in respect of growth performance. A larger firm may have slower growth because of its inability to react to changes in the market places as quickly as the small firms can. Equally, a larger firm may have a complex organisational structure making organisational change difficult to implement (Pant, 1991). It is equally true that an increase in firm's size may lead to difficulty in respect of co-ordination and control of various activities, diseconomies on account of idle capacity (Kaur, 1997). Our sample is made up of only larger companies, so growth might not be possible and desirable for a large sized firm on account of the factors narrated above. Hence, the larger size is associated with the lower growth. As regards the contribution of industry membership in explaining performance differentials, the impact of various industry categories on performance is in line with our findings of Chapter 5. However, the favourable effect of tobacco, paper, cotton textile and fertiliser industries on GRTH is contrary to the results of Chapter 5. This might be due to the omitted categories in our regression models (see Chapter 6 for details).

Summary and Conclusions

The purpose of this chapter has been to examine the relative roles played by market share, concentration and capacity utilisation in determining the performance of firms in Indian manufacturing industries. Additionally, industry dummy variables and certain other control variables have been used in the models to decompose the variation in performance. The performance has been administered in terms of firm-level profitability and growth. Hypothesis on market share predicted that it would be positively related to firm-level performance. Results indicate that market share is positive and significantly related to profitability and growth (however, not significant in all the models). Hence support was found for this hypothesis. Our second hypothesis predicted that industry concentration would be positively related to performance. Our results indicate that our predictions have failed to meet the hypothesis in both profitability and growth models.

While arguments have been presented for both, a positive and negative relationship in prior studies, the results of this study reveal a negative relationship between concentration and performance, perhaps due to the introduction of market share variable in the model. Many previous studies have reported the coefficient of concentration to be insignificant or negative when the model contained market share variable. The positive relationship revealed by some Indian studies might be due to the omission of market share variable in the model. Some support has been found for the third hypothesis which argued that capacity utilisation will be positively related to firm-level performance. The results indicate that higher utilisation of capacity enhances profitability.

8

CONCLUSIONS AND LOOKING AHEAD

Introduction

The Indian industry is becoming highly competitive and in competitive industries the strongest institutions survive and such institutions are ranked among the most efficient and effective ones. Success in competitive markets demands achieving the highest levels of performance through continuous improvement and feedback. It is, therefore, imperative that managers understand where they stand in relation to competitors. This study has investigated performance differences among various industries in India. The study has also sought to find the determinants of performance differentials.

Summary of Findings and Conclusions

This study has shown that inter-industry performance differentials are both statistically significant and quantitatively important mainly for Commodity/Activity-based classification of industries which defines industry at fairly disaggregate level of product grouping. The multiple regression models have revealed that industry effects account for a significant portion of the variance in rate of return and growth. The hypothesis of positive relationship between capital intensity and profitability is not supported. However, this has positive association with growth. If two companies have different degree of capital intensity but identical demand curves, marginal costs and average costs, the company with higher capital intensity will have lower profitability. Moreover, if a firm has built up plant of excess capacity right from the beginning, the idle capacity will depress profitability. Furthermore, firms with higher sunk costs may be compelled to remain in the business even if it is earning lower rate of returns because their close down will result in huge losses. As regards the positive relationship of this variable with growth, a firm with high capital intensity might have installed plant with excess capacity and it might be in a position to gear up its activities later on at a larger level due to its strong infrastructure.

Leverage has been found to have adverse impact on profitability while the same has positive relationship with growth. The possible explanation of the inverse relationship between leverage and profitability might be the interest cost associated with heavy debt load. A highly levered firm with its ROA lower than the cost of debt capital will naturally earn lower profits. This study has provided evidence of inverse relationship between profitability and risk. Higher risk results in lower performance, keeping the effects of other variables constant. This is contrary to economic theory which suggests that there will be excess returns associated with higher risk. The possible interpretation of inverse relationship between risk and profitability might be that highly profitable firms took the projects which involved lower risks. The risk in this study denotes some degree of financial fluctuation which can result from a variety of sources such as short term fluctuation in profits, changes in consumer tastes, changes in technology, changes in government policy, and strategic moves of competitors. The manager should take prompt actions to prevent or minimise the effect of these factors on profits of the firm. Risk and growth, however, are positively related. It shows that these firms were extra cautious to manage their risky projects which led to the favourable performance in terms of growth of these firms. In other words, risk bearing is compensated by a higher rate of growth.

Age had an adverse impact on performance probably due to the continuous use of outdated management and marketing practices and obsolete technology by the old firms. The inverse relationship between skill and growth may be on account of inefficiency of personnel, lack of co-operation and co-ordination among their activities, inflexibility to respond to changes in organisational structure. Further, use of ineffective or no personnel policy of the management may be the root cause of all these shortcomings.

The effect of size on profitability is positive in this study, though not significant in all the models. The positive relationship of size with profitability may be ascribed to scale economies; the larger the firm, the lower the cost of production and hence the higher profits. Firm size has been also considered as an important source of entry barriers. It may raise 'Capital requirement' barriers to entry and as such size distribution of firms may be taken to increase attainable profitability. The effect of this variable on growth in this study is negative (again not significant in all the models). The possible interpretation of this finding is that size causes X-inefficiency beyond a particular level. Apart from this, a larger firm may have slower growth because of its inability to react to changes in the market place as quickly as the smaller firms can. Equally, a large firm may have a complex organisation structure, making organisation change difficult to implement. However, without further evidence it cannot be inferred from this finding that big firms are subjected to diseconomies of scale.

The hypothesis of a positive influence of market share on performance is supported particularly for Commodity-based sample of industries. The positive association between market share and profits may be due to any or all the following reasons:

- Firms with large market share may be getting a market share based product differentiation advantage Firms with high market share may be able to satisfy customers' needs better and consequently be enjoying a competitive advantage *vis-à-vis* their smaller counterparts.
- A firm with large market share may be making higher profits due to the lower break-even point: the higher the sales, the higher the profits.
- Firms with large market shares may be producing goods of superior quality enabling them to charge higher prices than their small counterparts.
- Firms with a large share may be exploiting scale economies more efficiently.
- Companies with large market shares may be more innovative.

We find some support for the argument that greater utilisation of capacity results into higher profitability. Three conclusions can be drawn from this finding. First, higher costs and wastage due to underutilisation of existing capacity get reduced as a result of better utilisation of capacity, and in turn it would result in higher profitability and *vice versa*. Second, an increase in demand may entail the full exploitation of installed capacity and at the same time can enable the firm to charge higher prices, thus the higher capacity utilisation would result in higher profitability. Third, firms operating at higher capacity level may be availing economies of scale and hence higher margins.

Our results lend no support at all to the hypothesis that a firm protected in the market from competitive pressures by high concentration, exploit this position and earn an excessive rate of return. One possible explanation for this is that X-inefficiency arises for want of competition and is the result of inefficient use of assets and capital. The same goes on increasing along with increase in concentration to such an extent that it outweighs the effect on profits of the excess prices charged in the monopolistic industries. This is reflected in a low rate of return on assets and equity. Further, the finding that market share is significantly positive and concentration is significantly negative, can be taken to support the revisionist argument that efficiency differences, not collusion are the key to performance. Some studies have already provided evidences which challenge the traditional role of seller concentration as a determinant of profitability across industries. And market share rather than concentration has been shown as the primary determinant of profitability (Shepherd, 1972, 1979; Gale and Branch, 1982; Ravenscraft, 1983). This suggests that instead of mutual dependence among oligopolistic sellers, superiority in terms of better production, better management, lower costs etc. are more important.

Implications

Studies, such as this, could help us find the factors responsible for poor performance of certain industries and guide the formulation of strategies to remove the disparities among industries. The government should not make uniform policies for all the industries. For example, from amongst the segments of Input-based industry classification, the Agro-based industries are the most vulnerable to monsoons (excess or dearth), droughts etc. The policies should contain special provisions to provide such industries protection and incentives in the form of tax holdings, subsidies and/or the like.

From the investors' and entrepreneurs' viewpoints, the investment in iron and steel, paints, pharmaceutical, sugar and tyre and tube industries may be stated to be the most beneficial as these industries are good on both the profitability and the growth dimension of performance. The existing companies may reduce their risk by expanding or diversifying their operations in these industries. Creditors and lenders can also visualise these industries as the most potential area to invest in as they always want to get the interest regularly and the return of their principal at maturity. They can also visualise that the higher profitability and growth can certainly contribute to make the solvency position of the firm stronger. Finally, the managements of the firms functioning in these industry groups may feel at ease as they have to protect the interests of shareholders (who concentrate on profitability) and see simultaneously that the companies grow profitability. The conclusion which can be drawn from the findings on age variable, is that the old firms should keep on updating their management and marketing practices as well as the technology in the light of the changes in the business world. The adverse impact of expenditure on salary and wages of personnel can be prevented by making sound personal policy by the management. Today it has been realised that human resource is the most important asset in any organisation. Its neglect can render the huge investment on even the most sophisticated technology to be fruitless.

The unfavourable impact of leverage on profitability can be avoided by reducing the dependability on debt capital, particularly when the business does not produce a rate of return at least equivalent to rate of interest to be paid on borrowed capital. The managers can draw the lesson from the evidence on market share that increase of business' market share improves performance of the business. But the best strategy may not always be to increase market share. It should be kept in mind that if high market share ushers high profitability, gaining of market share might also entail heavy investment which may, in turn, cause negative results in the short run. Hence, the implication of the conclusion that market share has been a determinant of performance should not be given too much emphasis in planning and strategy on market share. Other fundamentals can be of equal or greater importance. More emphasis might be placed upon such key areas as product quality, customer satisfaction, productivity, corporate culture, product line appropriateness, and management effectiveness. In fact, situations could exist where a decline in market share may actually be an indication of good management. Efforts to keep or gain market share, for the sake of being number one or having a certain market share rank, may have a detrimental impact on ROI both in short and long run.

If the validity of the findings on concentration-performance relationship is accepted, their implication is that policies designed to reduce concentration will neither lead to any improvements in productivity nor they will remove any excess profit as there is no excess profit in our case. With regard to capacity utilisation, the implication for the managers, entrepreneurs and the State can be that they should install as much capacity for the production as can be utilised in a better way presently or in the near future. The establishment of excess capacity will remain idle causing unnecessary blockage of capital and fruitless addition to costs.

Finally, in the light of the above-mentioned implications, two precautionary points must be stated precisely. Firstly, the findings of this study cannot be taken as conclusive because performance is a complex phenomenon and it is influenced by a number of factors. Here only some of these have been taken into consideration in this thesis. Secondly, the estimation results might be sensitive to data sample. It had been witnessed that when results were taken with the truncated data sample, changes occurred with regard to the intensity of coefficients and explanatory power of the model. This suggests that underlying data might be the root of disagreement in empirical results taken by different researchers though using identical or very similar model specifications.

Scope for Further Research

During the research we thought of many ideas but found them not worth trying in this study because we had reached quite an advance stage of the work. Moreover, information for some variables became available after our study period. We hope it would enhance the scope:

(1) in making inter-sectoral and inter-temporal comparisons of results which in turn, may reveal new relationships among various variables used in this study;
(2) in identifying variables that could be employed to better explain the variation in performance. Such a study of performance requires that research and development expenditure, advertising intensity, import and export ratios, strategy and structure of the business be included in it in particular;
(3) in undertaking a study by making use of other data basis and other regression models especially the ones which include interaction effects of various variables; and
(4) in concentrating upon a study of inter-industry performance analysis by using an industry classification which defines industry at more disaggregate level, i.e. product level.

Finally, this study has analysed performance differentials and interpreted results thereof with the help of ANOVA, factor analysis, multiple regression equations etc. However, the recent developments and extension of frontier estimation research has enhanced computational feasibility by developing various computer software techniques which can provide deeper insights into inter-industry performance differentials and the causes thereof. But the same could not find a place in this study because of the structure of this study. Some of such techniques are benchmarking, Total Quality Management (TQM), Data Envelopment Analysis

(DEA) etc., the application of these techniques can open up a wide range of new possibilities and directions for research. Benchmarking is an effective technique which can provide breakthrough for significant improvements and can alert institutions to new practices and new paradigms. Benchmarking can be undertaken to compare the firm(s)/industry(ies) with other firm(s)/industry(ies) in order to identify areas of improvement. Comparison can be done across various performance indicators like profitability, productivity, growth as well as with regard to various other firm/industry characteristics like size, R&D, capital structure, capacity utilisation etc. Benchmarking searches for best practices to improve a firm's/industry's performance, for instance that size or that level of capacity utilisation can be found where the firm/industry performs the best. And once the best practices are identified and understood, action plans can be formulated for improvement. Data envelopment analysis (DEA) is another way to analyse data. It can be used to analyse best practices and compute relative strengths and weakness. The mathematical programming approach of DEA is a robust procedure for efficient frontier estimations. In contrast to statistical procedures based on central tendencies, DEA focuses on the revealed best practice frontiers. That is, DEA analyses each unit (may it be a firm or an industry) separately, thereafter it measures relative performance with respect to the entire population being evaluated. Total quality management (TQM) is another very popular technique for total organisational development. TQM is a continuous approach to develop quality in all facets of organisation, be it financial or non-financial, human or non-human. It encompasses within itself all activities designed to achieve effectiveness and efficiency. TQM is very scientific and rigorous, as it revolves around documenting each activity and improving each one of them by introducing standardisation and precision.

BIBLIOGRAPHY

Aggarwal, A.K. (1992), *Performance Variation Across Industries: Role of Ownership, Trade and Market Structure*, A Dissertation Submitted in Partial Fulfilment of the Requirements for the Fellow Programme in Management, the Indian Institute of Management, Ahmedabad.

Ahluwalia, I.J. (1985), *Industrial Growth in India*, Oxford University Press, Delhi.

Amato, L. and Wilder, R.P. (1990), "Firm and Industry Effects in Industrial Economics", *Southern Economic Journal*, 50(1): 93-105.

Amjad, R. (1977), "Profitability and Industrial Concentration in Pakistan", *Journal of Development Studies*, 13(3): 181-198.

Arditti, F.D. (1967), "Risk and the Required Return on Equity", *Journal of Finance*, 22 (March): 19-36.

Armour, H.O. and Teece, D. (1978), "Organisational Structure and Economic Performance: A Test of Multidivisional Hypothesis", *Bell Journal of Economics*, 9 (Spring) : 106-122.

Bain, J.S. (1951), "Relation of Profit Rate to Industry Concentration: American Manufacturing, 1936-1940", *Quarterly Journal of Economics*, 65 (August): 293-324.

Bain, J.S. (1956), *Barriers to New Competition*, Cambridge; Harvard University Press.

Bain, J.S. (1968), *Industrial Organisation*, 2nd. ed. New York: John Wiley and Sons, Inc.

Bajaj, B.K. (1977-78), *Capacity Utilization in Bicycle Industry (complete Bicycle) in Ludhiana*, Unpublished thesis of M.Phil. in Economics, Panjab University, Chandigarh.

Baker, S.H. (1973), "Risk, Leverage and Profitability—an Industry Analysis", *The Review of Economics and Statistics*, 55(4): 503-507.

Barna, T. (1962), *Investment and Growth Policies in British Industrial Firms*, Cambridge University Press, Cambridge.

Berle, A.A. and Means, G.C. (1932), *The Modern Corporation and Private Property*, New York, Mcmillan.

Bettis, R.A. (1981), "Performance Differences in Related and Unrelated Diversified Firms", *Strategic Management Journal*, 2: 379-393.

Bettis, R.A. and Hall, W.K. (1982), Diversification Strategy, Accounting Determined Risk and Accounting Determined Return, *Academy of Management Journal*, 25(2): 254-64.

Bothwell, J.L. and Others (1984), "A new view of the market structure-market performance debate", *Journal of Industrial Economics*, 32: 397-417.

Bourgeois, L.J. (1980), "Performance and Consensus", *Strategic Management Journal*, 1:227-248.

Bourgeois, L.J. (1985), "Strategic Goals, Perceived Uncertainty, and Economic Performance in Volatile Environments", *Academy of Management Journal*, 28(3):548-573.

Bowman, E.H. (1980), "A risk/return paradox for strategic management", *Sloan Management Review*, 21(3): 17-31.

Branch, Ben S. (1980), "The Laws of Market Place and ROI Dynamics", *Financial Management*, (Summer): 58-65.

Brozen, Y. (1970), "The Antitrust Task Force Deconcentration Recommendations", *Journal of Law and Economics*, 13:279-292.

Capon, N. and Others (1988), "Corporate Diversity and Economic Performance: The Impact of Market Specialisation", *Strategic Management Journal*, 9:61-74.

Carleton, W.T. and Silberman, I.H. (1977), "Joint Determination of Rate of Return and Capital Structure: An Econometric Analysis", *Journal of Finance*, 811-21.

Carter, J.R. (1978), "Collusion, Efficiency, and Antitrust", *Journal of Law and Economics*, 21 (October): 435-444.

Catry, B. and Chevalie, M. (1974), "Market Share Strategy and the Product Life Cycle", *Journal of Marketing*, (October): 29-34.

Caves, R.E. (1974), "Causes of direct investment: Foreign firms shares in Canadian and United Kingdom manufacturing industries", *Review of Economics and Statistics*, 56(3).

Chaganti, R. and Damanpour, F. (1991), "Institutional Ownership Capital Structure, and Firm Performance", *Strategic Management Journal*, 12:479-491.

Chamberlin, Edward M. (1962), *The Theory of Monpolistic Competition*, 8th ed. Cambridge: Harvard University Press (Original edition, 1933).

Chandler, A.D. (1962), *Strategy and Structure—Chapters in the History of American Industrial Enterprise*, Cambridge Mass., The MIT Press.

Chappel, W. and Cottle, R. (1985), "Sources of Concentration related profit", *Southern Economic Journal*, 51(April): 1031-1037.

Chhibber, P. and Majumdar, S.K. (1998), "State as Investor and State as Owner: Consequences for Firm Performance in India", *Economic Development and Cultural Change*, Vol. 46, No. 3, pp. 561-580.

Coate, M.B. (1989), "The Dynamics of Price-Cost Margins in Concentrated Industries," *Applied Economics*, 21:261-272.

Coate, M.B. and Uri, N.D. (1988), "A Simultaneous Equations Approach to Modelling Industry Structure and Economic Performance", *Metro Economica*, XXXIX (2):181-204.

Connor, J.M. and Mueller, W.F. (1982), "Market Structure and Performance of US multinationals in Brazil and Mexico", *Journal of Development Studies*, 18(3):329-353.

Cubbin, J. and Geroski, P.A. (1987), "The Convergence of Profits in the long run: Inter-firm and inter-industry comparisons", *The Journal of Industrial Economics*, 35(4): 427-442.

Dalton, J.A. and Penn, D.W. (1976), "The Concentration Profitability Relationship: Is There a Critical Concentration Ratio?", *The Journal of Industrial Economics*, XXV (2): 133-142.

Demsetz, H. (1973), "Industry Structure, Market Rivalry and Public Policy", *Journal of Law and Economics*, 16 (April):1-10.

Devine, P.J., Lee, N., Jones, R.M. and Tyson, W.T. (1979), *An Introduction to Industrial Economics*, Third edition, George Allen and Unwin Ltd., 40, Museum Street, London WCIA ILU.

Fisher, I.N. and Hall, G.R. (1969), "Risk and Corporate rates of return", *Quarterly Journal of Economics*, 83 (February): 79-92.

Fox, J. (1984), *Linear Statistical Models and Related Methods*, John Wiley and Sons.

Gale, B.T. (1972), "Market Share and Rate of Return", *The Review of Economics and Statistics*, 54(4): 412-423.

Gale, Bradley T. and Branch, Ben S. (1982), "Concentration Versus Market Share: Which Determines Performance and Why Does It Matter?", *Antitrust Bulletin* 27 (Spring): 83-106.

Gan, W.B. (1978), "The relationship between market concentration and profitability in Malaysian Manufacturing Industries", *Malayan Economic Review*, 23(1):1-13.

Gan, W.B. and Tham, S.Y. (1977), "Market Structure and Price-Cost Margin in Malaysian Manufacturing Industries", *The Development Economics*, 15(3): 280-292.

Grant, M. and Jammine, A.P. (1988), "Performance Differences between the Wrigley/Rumelt Strategic Categories", *Strategic Management Journal*, 9:333-346.

Gujrati, Damodar, N. (1995), *Basic Econometrics*, 3rd. ed., McGraw Hill International Editions.

Gupta, V.K. (1968), "Cost Functions Concentration, and Barrier to Entry in Twenty-Nine Manufacturing Industries of India", *Journal of Industrial Economics*, 26(1) : 57-72.

Gupta, Meena and Thavaraj, M.J.K. (1975), "Capacity Utilization and Profitability: A Case Study of Fertilizer Units", *Productivity*, 16(3); 882-892.

Hall, M. and Weiss, L. (1967), "Firm Size and Profitability", *Review of Economics and Statistics*, 49(3): 319-331.

Hamilton, R.T. and Shergill, G.S. (1993), *The Logic of New Zealand Business*, Oxford University Press, Auckland.

Hardy, M.A. (1993) "Regression with Dummy Variables", pp. 69-158 in Michael S. Lewis-Beck (ed.) *International Handbooks of Quantitative Applications in the Social Sciences*, Vol. 2, Regression Analysis, Sage Publication, Toppan Publishing.

Harris, F.H. Deb (1986), "Market Structure and Price Cost Performance under endogenous profit risk", *Journal of Industrial Economics*, 35: 35-60.

Harrod, R.F. (1933-34), "Doctrines of Imperfect Competition", *Quarterly Journal of Economics*; 48 (3) : 442-70.

Hirschey, M. (1985), "Market Structure and Market Value", *Journal of Business*, 58:89-98.

Holtermann, S.E. (1973), "Market Struture and Economic Performance in U.K. Manufacturing Industry", *The Journal of Industrial Economics*, (December) : 119-39.

House, W.J. (1973), "Market Structure and Industry Performance: The Case of Kenya," *Oxford Economic Papers*, 25(3):117-132.

House, W.J. (1976), "Market Structure and Industry Performance: the case of Kenya Revisited", *Journal of Economic Studies*, 3(2): 117-32.

Jacobson, R. and Aaker, D.A. (1985), "Is Market Share all its Cracked up to be?", *Journal of Marketing*, 49 (Fall):11-22.

Jensen, M. (1989), "The eclipse of the public corporation", *Harward Business Review*, 67: 61-74.

Jeong, K.Y. and Masson, R.T. (1990), "Market Structure Entry, and Performance in Korea", *The Review of Economics and Statistics*, LXXII(3): 455-62.

Jones,T.T. and Cockrill, T.A.J. (1985), *Structure and Performance of Industries*, Heritage Publishers, New Delhi-2.

Katrak, H. (1980), "Industrial Structure, Foreign Trade and Price-Cost Margins in Indian Manufacturing Industries", *Journal of Development Studies*, 17(1): 62-79.

Kaur, Parminder (1992), "Capacity Utilisation in Indian Industry : An Empirical Analysis," Unpublished Ph.D. thesis submitted to Guru Nanak Dev University, Amritsar, Punjab.

Kaur, Kuldip (1997), *Size, Growth and Profitability of Firms,* Gyan Publishing House, New Delhi-2.

Kessides, I.N. (1990), "Internal versus External Markets—Conditions and Firm Profitability : An Exploratory Model", *The Economic Journal*, 100(Sept.) : 773-92.

Kirkpatrick, C.H.; Lee, N. and Nixson, F.I. (1985), *Industrial Structure and Policy in Less Developed Countries*, Heritage Publishers, New Delhi-2.

Kleinbaum, David G., Kupper, Lawrence L., and Muller, Keith E. (1988), *Applied Regression Analysis and Other Multivariate Methods*, 2nd ed., Pins-Kent, Boston, Mass.

Kumar, P. (1985), *Growth of Industrial Corporation in India*, Deep and Deep Publications, New Delhi-27.

Levy, D.T. (1984), "Variation in the Concentration—Profit Relationship Across Industries", *Southern Economic Journal*, 51(1):267-273.

Lindsey, C.W. (1977), "Market Concentration in Philippines Manufacturing, 1970", *Philippines Economic Journal*, 16(3): 289-312.

Maharatna, A. (1983), "Change in Concentration and Growth in Indian Industries 1964-80", *The Indian Economic Journal*, 37(2):93-102.

Mann, H.M. (1966), "Seller Concentration, Barriers to Entry and Rates of Return in 30 Industries", *The Review of Economics and Statistics*, 48(3): 296-307.

Marcus, M. (1969), "Profitability and Size of Firms : Some Further Evidence", *The Review of Economics and Statistics,* 51:104-107.

Masuda, T. (1993), "Competitivity of the Japanese Highly Concentrated Industries—The Chicago School's Approach", *Economic Journal of Hokkaido University,* 22: 131-146.

McEnally, R.W. (1976), "Competition and Dispersion in Rates of Return: A Note", *Journal of Industrial Organisation*, 25(September): 69-75.

Meehan, James, W.JR. and Duchesneau, T.D. (1973), "The Critical Level of Concentration : An Empirical Analysis", *The Journal of Industrial Economics*, XXII(1): 21-36.

Millward, R. (1982), *The Comparative Performance of Public and Private Ownership*, in *The Mixed Economy*, edited by Lord Roll of Ipsden, Macmillan Press, pp.58-93.

Mishra, R.K. (1977), "Capacity Utilization in Durgapur Steel Plant", *Eastern Economist*, 69 (3):119-125.

Montgomery, C.A. (1979), *Diversification, Market Structure and Firm Performance : an Extension of Rumelt's Model*, Ph.D. dissertation, Purdue University.

Montgomery, C.A. (1985), "Product-market Diversification and Market Power", *Academy of Management Journal*, 28:789-798.

Nam, W.H. (1975), "The Determinants of Industrial Concentration : The Case of Korea", *Malayan Economic Review*, 20(1): 37-48.

Neter, J. and Wasserman, W. (1974), *Applied Linear Statistical Models*, Homewood, Illinois: Richard D. Irwin.

Neter, J., Wasserman, W. and Kunter, M.H. (1989), *Applied Linear Regression Models*, Homewood, Illinois, Richard D. Irwin.

Neumann, M., Bobel, I. and Haid, A. (1979), "Profitability, Risk and Market Structure in West German Industries", *Journal of Industrial Economics*, 27(3):227-242.

Neumann, M. and Others (1985), "Domestic Concentration, Foreign Trade and Economic Performance", *International Journal of Industrial Organisation*, 3: 1-19.

Newfarmer, R.S. and Mueller, W.F. (1975), *Multinational Corporation in Brazil and Mexico : Structural Sources of Economic and Non-Economic Power*, (Washington, DC:US Senate Sub-committee on Multinational Corporations).

Orr, D. (1974), "The Determinants of Entry : A Study of the Canadian Manufacturing Industries", *Review of Economics and Statistics*, 56(I):58-66.

Orr, D. (1974^A), "An Index of Entry Barriers and its Application to the Structure Performance Relationship", *Journal of Industrial Economics,* 23(1): 39-50.

Pant, L.W. (1991), "An Investigation of Industry and Firm Structural Characteristics in Corporate Turnarounds", *Journal of Management Studies*, 28(6): 623-43.

Peltzman, S. (1977), "The Gains and Losses from Industrial Concentration", *Journal of Law and Economics*, 20 (October): 229-64.

Penrose, E.T. (1959), *The Theory of Growth of Firm*, London Basil Black.

Phillips, A. (1976), "A Critic of Empirical Studies of Relations between Market Structure and Profitability", *Journal of Industrial Economics,* XXIV(4):241-249.

Pittie, M.N. (1975), "Utilization of Idle Capacity in Sugar Industry", *Indian Sugar,* 25 (7) : 611-62.

Porter, M.E. (1976), *Interbrand Choice, Strategy and Bilateral Market Power*, Cambridge : Harvard University Press.

Porter, M.E. (1979), "The Structure Within Industries and Companies Performance", *Review of Economics and Statistics*, 61(2) : 214-28.

Porter, M.E. (1980), *Competitive Strategy*, The Free Press, New York.

Porter, M.E. (1985), *Competitive Advantage,* Free Press, New York.

Ramappa, C.M.M. (1970), "Effect of Idle Capacity on Industrial Productivity", *The Indian Journal of Commerce*, 23 (84):40-50.

Ravenscraft, D.J. (1983), "Structure-Profit Relationship at the Line of Business and Industry Level", *Review of Economics and Statistics,* 65:22-31.

Reekie, W.D. (1984), "The Structure-Conduct-Performance Paradigm in a South African Setting", *The South African Journal of Economics*, 52(2):146-155.

Rhoades, S.A. (1973), "The Effect of Diversification on Industry Profit Performance in 241 Manufacturing Industries 1963", *The Review of Economics and Statistics*, 55(2): 146-155.

Rumelt, R.P. (1974), *Strategy, Structure, and Economic Performance*, Cambridge Mass, Harvard University Press.

Rumelt, R.P. (1977), *Diversity and Profitability*, Working paper MGL-51. Managerial Studies Centre, Graduate School of Management, University of California, Los Angeles.

Rumelt, R.P. (1982), *How Important is Industry in Explaining Firm Profitability?"* Unpublished Working Paper, UCLA.

Rumelt, R.P. (1991), "How Much Does Industry Matter?" *Strategic Management Journal,* 12: 167-185.

Rummel, R.J. (1970), *Applied Factor Analysis*, Evanston, Northwestern University Press.

Satyanarayana, J. and Sarma, K.R.K. (1979), "Capacity Utilization in Public Enterprises in India", *Indian Journal of Commerce*, 32 (118):9-21.

Sawhney, P.K. and Sawhney, B.L. (1973), "Capacity-Utilization, Concentration, and Price-Cost Margins : Results on Indian

Industries", *Journal of Industrial Economics*, 21(2):145-153.

Schmalensee, R. (1985), "Do Markets Differ Much?", *The American Economic Review*, 75(1): 341-51.

Schmalensee, R. (1989), "Inter-Industsry Studies of Structure and Performance", in *Handbook of Industrial Organisation"*, edited by R.Schmalensee and R. Willig, Amsterdam: North Holland.

Schwalbach, J. (1991), "Profitability and Market Share : A Reflection on the Functional Relationship", *Strategic Management Journal*, 12:279-306.

Scott, J.T. and Pascoe, G. (1986), "Beyond Firm and Industry Effects on Profitability in Imperfect Markets", *The Review of Economics and Statistics*, 68(2): 248-92.

Sharwani, K. (1976), "Some New Evidence on Concentration and Profitability in Pakistan's Large Scale Manufacturing Industries", *Pakistan Development Review*, 15(3): 272-289.

Shepherd, W.G. (1972), "Elements of Market Structure", *The Review of Economics and Statistics*, 54(1): 25-37.

Shepherd, W.G. (1979), *The Economics of Industrial Organization*, Prentice Hall Inc., Englewood Cliffs, N.J.

Siddharthan, N.S. and Dasgupta, A.K. (1983), "Entry Barriers, Exports and Inter-Industry Differences in Profitability", *The Developing Economics*, 21(1): 14-23.

Sidhu, H.S. and Bhatia, G. (1993), "Factors Affecting Profitability in Indian Textile Industry", *The Indian Economic Journal*, 41 (2) : 137-143.

Stigler, G.J. (1964), A Theory of Oligopoly, *Journal of Political Economy*, 72:44-61.

Wagner, H.M. (1984), "Profit Wonders, Investment Blunder", *Harvard Business Review*, 62(October): 121-35.

Walgreen, J.A. (1971), "Cost Functions, Concentration and Barriers to Entry in Twenty-nine Manufacturing Industries in India : A Comment and Re-interpretation", *Journal of Industrial Economics*, 20(1): 90-95.

Weiss, L.W. (1974), "The Concentration—Profit Relationship and Antitrust", in : H.J. Goldschmid, H.M. Mann and J.F. Weston, eds, *Industrial Concentration : The New Learning*, Boston : Little Brown.

Weiss, L.W. (1991), *Structure, Conduct and Performance* (Edited by Avdretsch, D.B. and Yamaawaki, H.), Harvester Wheatsheaf, Hertfordshire HPZ, 4RG.

White, L.J. (1974), *Industrial Concentration and Economic Power in Pakistan*, Princeton: Princeton University Press.

Woo, C.Y. and Cooper, A.C. (1982), "The Surprising Case for low market share", *Harvard Business Review*, 60 (November-December): 106-13.

Zaltman, Gerald and Burger, Phillip (1975), *Marketing Research : Fundamentals and Dynamics,* Dryden Press, Hinsdale.

INDEX